Building Data Products

The Data Products Series
Volume 2

Mario Meir-Huber

Technics Publications
SEDONA, ARIZONA

TECHNICS PUBLICATIONS

115 Linda Vista, Sedona, AZ 86336 USA
https://www.TechnicsPub.com

Edited by Steve Hoberman
Cover design by Lorena Molinari

First Printing 2026

ISBN, print ed. 9798898161453
ISBN, Kindle ed. 9798898161460
ISBN, PDF ed. 9798898161477

Library of Congress Control Number: 2026946439

Contents

Foreword

Where Does a Data Product Exist?

In *The Data Product Series, Volume 2: Building Data Products*, Mario Meir-Huber provides us with a field guide for Data Products. The fundamental question asked in the opening pages of the book is where a Data Product exists.

And it is exactly the answer to that question that motivates Mario to put these ideas forward and gather them into a book. Because a Data Product is, holistically speaking, not in one place. Of course, the logical, intuitive approach is to think of a Data Product as something that is stored somewhere, in a database.

However, the nature of metadata is at play: the Data Product is in multiple places at once. It sits in a database, and it lives as a metadata representation in a data catalog. The catalog is where the Data Product is described, tagged, controlled, and managed throughout its lifecycle.

This fact, that the Data Product exists in several places at the same time, is why companies are in need of data ownership. Mario addresses the need for the organization to move as one: it is precisely the split in the where and the how of Data Products that is hindering the organization from moving as one. The GAP triad of Governance, Architecture, and People is split across retrieving data, building pipelines, providing business context, and much more. The need is to make everyone come together so that enterprise Data Products actually become a success. Pipelines can run perfectly, but they will create chaos if responsibilities are unclear, standards are optional, or no one is accountable for long-term quality.

Everyone working in tech knows that marketing buzzwords dominate hype cycles: flimsy, sometimes even dubious concepts are launched to be on top of the trends and capture attention. It is a particular pleasure for me to read this book, as someone who followed the data mesh movement from the very early days until the data mesh concept faded. At the ultimate peak of the data mesh movement, sometime in 2022 and early 2023, the number of buzzwords around data mesh was unsettling and confusing.

This book is the opposite of that. Mario writes with true industry experience about the idea that remained from the data mesh movement: the Data Product. It is very clear to see in the specific examples throughout the book that the identified challenge is real, needs to be solved, and can indeed be solved with his approach. In particular, Mario's explanations of how to apply the Bitol standards are extraordinarily clear and convincing.

The advice laid out in the following pages is concrete and applicable. To succeed with Data Products, I suggest you follow it. The key is to ask yourself, "Where does the Data Product exist?"

Ole Olesen-Bagneux, PhD Chief Evangelist, Actian

Introduction

In Volume 1, we did something important. We stopped treating data as a side effect of projects and started treating it as a product. As a real product with consumers, expectations, and a lifecycle.

This matters because most organizations do not fail due to missing data. They fail because data is hard to trust, hard to find, hard to reuse, and hard to maintain. Volume 1 gave us a way out of that trap. Now, at the start of Volume 2, we align on the shared language again, before we dive deep into building Data Products. In case you just finished Volume 1 of this series, you can skip this intro chapter. This chapter is for those who finished Volume 1 some weeks to months ago or didn't read it at all.

Defining Data Products

We learned that a Data Product is only a Data Product if it delivers value to its consumers. That statement sounds simple, but it is strong. A dataset that nobody uses is not a product. A dashboard that cannot be trusted is not a product. A pipeline that breaks is not a product. While we discuss a general definition here, we will look at a technical definition later in this book.

So, we adopted a product mindset. We asked who the consumers are, what they need, and how the Data Product proves over time that it still delivers value. This is the big shift that separates Data Products from classic deliverables. When we talk about Data Projects, we talk about the challenging things that somehow accidentally make it into production and then remain there unnoticed for many years. A Data Product requires constant maintenance because it is never finished. Business environments constantly change and while a Data Project only receives "quick fixes", this ever-changing environment is part of each Data Product.

Now let's revisit the key attributes that make up a proper Data Product:

- **Clear purpose and consumer relevance**: A Data Product must serve a clear purpose for a defined group of consumers. If it does not create value for its users, it should be treated as irrelevant and discontinued, just as unused reports become "Data Product antiques."

- **Usability and readiness**: A Data Product must be easy to use within its domain and ready for real consumption. It must also be easy to discover and access, and it must clearly explain what it is, what it contains, and how it should be used.

- **Reliability and transparency**: A Data Product must be reliable so users can make decisions without second-guessing the numbers. It must also be transparent about correctness and creation, because trust erodes quickly when data is wrong or cannot be explained.

- **Understandable and self describing**: A Data Product must describe itself, so users understand what the data represents without needing manual interpretation. This requires clear descriptions, self-explanatory fields where possible, and explicit definitions for KPIs and business terms in plain language.

- **Approved and up to date**: A Data Product needs an accountable owner and active lifecycle management to remain relevant and current. That includes an approval process for bringing it into production and for retiring it when it becomes outdated or irrelevant.

- **Composable and interoperable**: Data Products are often built on top of other Data Products, which only works if they can be combined reliably. This requires shared standards and consistency; otherwise, composability breaks down, and products become isolated assets.

- **Trustworthy, secure, and reliable**: A Data Product must provide accurate data and operate reliably; otherwise, it can lead to wrong decisions, even if everything else looks good. It must also be secure, because Data Products can contain sensitive information and power critical business processes.

- **Discoverable and addressable**: A Data Product that cannot be found will not be used, regardless of its quality. Discoverability must be paired with technical addressability, meaning there is a concrete way to access and consume the product after it has been discovered.

- **Shared platform and models**: Platforms and data models must be shared to maximize reuse and efficiency across teams. This avoids competing ingestion routes and multiple models representing the same entity, which would otherwise lead to inconsistencies and rework.

- **Robust**: A Data Product must handle failures of components and dependencies as a normal part of reality. Robustness requires engineering discipline, so the product does not collapse when upstream systems or dependent Data Products fail.

- **Data quality and integrity management**: Data quality is a first-class requirement because a Data Product without quality does not deliver value. Quality and integrity must be managed thoroughly, because otherwise the Data Product becomes a liability for the business.

- **Monitoring and observability**: Data Products require proactive monitoring and alerting to detect issues early and prevent silent impacts on consumers. Without observability, teams cannot reliably identify root causes, and the Data Product becomes an unmanaged business risk.

The Data Product process

In Volume 1, we introduced a process for how data flows. Figure 1 shows this process.

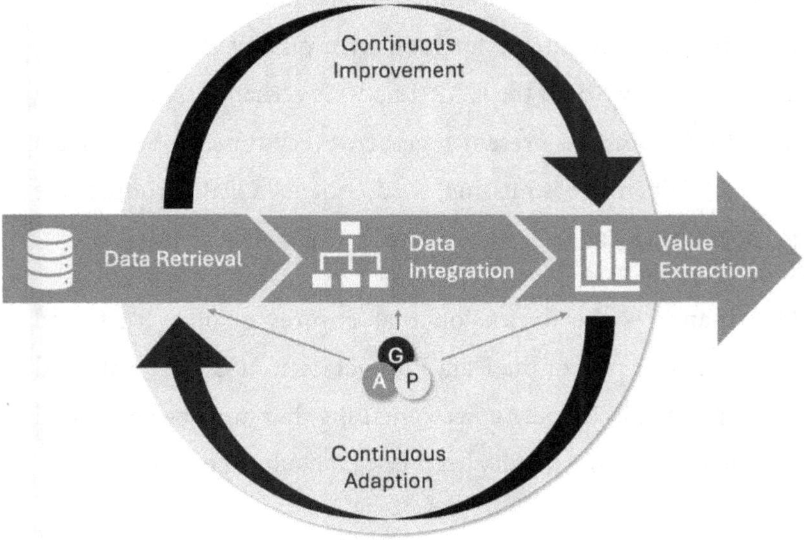

Figure 1: The Data Product process.

The key difference with Data Projects is that data is constantly in motion, and Data Products need to account for this challenge. We don't develop a pipeline or Data Project and then "forget about it" until it breaks in production. We constantly rebuild and repurpose until we can retire a Data Product. There are three key concepts to this in the above illustration: GAP (**G**overnance, **A**rchitecture, and **P**eople), DRIVE **(D**ata **R**etrieval to **I**ntegration, and eventually how **V**alue is **E**xtracted), and CIA (**C**ontinuous **I**mprovement and **A**daptation).

GAP

We learned quickly that Data Products do not fail because teams are not smart enough. They fail because the organization does not move as one. We can build excellent pipelines and still create chaos if responsibilities are unclear, standards are optional, or nobody feels accountable for long-term quality. This is why we anchored our work in the GAP Triad. Governance, Architecture, and People must be present together, every time, in every Data Product. When one is missing, we do not get a Data Product. We get something fragile.

Governance is the dimension that ensures quality, trust, and compliance as part of the Data Product itself. It is not positioned as a separate discipline, but as something that must be embedded into delivery so that quality becomes a default expectation.

A Data Product without quality does not deliver value, and governance is therefore a necessary ingredient for real outcomes, even if it is often underestimated in organizations.

Architecture is the technical backbone for robustness and scalability, and it goes beyond selecting tools. It covers the concrete mechanisms that make a Data Product usable in practice, such as well-defined access mechanisms, interfaces like APIs, and the technical implementation of ownership and process. It also includes shared platforms and shared data models to prevent competing ingestion routes and inconsistent representations of the same entity, which directly affects speed, reuse, and long-term quality.

People and culture determine whether Data Products are adopted and sustained, making them a core pillar, not a soft add-on. We defined that even the best tools, platforms, and governance structures fail if people resist using them, and that business value requires active stakeholder integration. It also emphasizes ownership and training, because reducing resistance, building understanding, and enabling new ways of working are prerequisites for continuous improvement over the lifecycle of a Data Product.

DRIVE

Building Data Products requires a process just like an assembly line. In Volume 1, we introduced DRIVE. This assembly line takes us consistently from raw inputs to a usable product. We also made one thing non-negotiable: in every step of this framework, the GAP triad comes into play. These three aspects are relevant from day one and must not be added later when it is too late.

Drive starts with Data Retrieval. We start by defining which data we need and for what purpose, because retrieval without a clear goal creates noise and waste. We then bring data from a broad range of systems and formats into the Data Product, while acknowledging that enterprise sourcing is heterogeneous and often inconsistent. We choose between real-time retrieval and batch processing, understanding the trade-offs among freshness, cost, and engineering complexity. We protect quality at the very beginning, and we handle deltas efficiently with CDC techniques. We explicitly manage upstream dependencies, often via DAGs, and treat retrieved assets as input ports that must be checked against their contracts.

Next comes Integration. Once data is retrieved, we structure, transform, enrich, and aggregate it so it becomes usable for the intended consumers, as most transformations occur in this phase. We use patterns like the Medallion architecture to make the maturity of data explicit and to decouple requirements across stages: Bronze stays close to the source, Silver adds cleaning, validation, and model alignment, and Gold delivers business-ready data for the visible part of the Data Product. We also distinguish how deeply we integrate based on the product's inner layout, where source-aligned products may stay close to Bronze or Silver, while consumer-aligned products typically reach Gold. We rely on modeling choices across layers, and we choose the modeling strategy based on purpose. We also avoid redundant processing by building consumer-aligned products on top of existing source-aligned and aggregated layers to improve consistency and KPI alignment, and we treat ownership and shared accountability as part of integration.

We complete DRIVE with Value Extraction. This last phase ensures the Data Product delivers measurable business value, because without this step, we only built a pipeline, not a product. We put the data into action by exposing it through concrete output ports that stakeholders can use, such as dashboards, APIs, machine learning models, MCP-based AI use, or operational integrations. We make accessibility explicit, but we also separate it from usability, because access alone does not create impact. We provide clear documentation, so the product is self-explanatory, and we upskill users through training to reduce resistance and enable real adoption. This is the point where the Data Product becomes visible, usable, and impactful, and where return on investment is determined.

CIA

Too many Data Projects are one-off developments that then run forever in production. Often, no one notices them until things break. This is never good, and thus, Data Products require a continuous process.

CIA is where Data Products stop being a delivery and start becoming a living capability. We do not ship and forget. We continuously integrate new requirements, new sources, and improvements into the product while actively driving adoption so usage grows rather than fades. We measure how the product is used, we listen to feedback, and we turn signals into concrete iterations that strengthen trust, quality, and relevance. CIA keeps the Data Product aligned with reality, so it stays valuable even as the business, data, and organization keep changing.

How to use this book

Volume 1 was about understanding what Data Products are and why they matter. This book is about starting to build them.

If you have read Volume 1, you already know the frameworks: the GAP triad, the DRIVE lifecycle, and the principles that separate Data Products from Data Projects. If it has been a while, or if you skipped Volume 1 entirely, the Intro chapter that follows will get you up to speed. It recaps the shared language we need before we start building.

This book focuses on one phase of the DRIVE framework: Data Retrieval. That might sound narrow, but retrieval is where most Data Products succeed or fail. It is the point where your product meets reality: messy source systems, unclear ownership, inconsistent schemas, and the organizational friction that comes with pulling data from systems that were never designed to share it. Getting retrieval right requires governance, architecture, and people working together from day one, and that is exactly what this book delivers.

Compared to Volume 1, this book is lighter on standalone stories of failures and successes. We jump more directly into the topic, though you will still find experiences from my own practice that help.

Here is what you will find in this book:

- Chapter 1 establishes the technical foundation. We introduce the Open Data Product Standard (ODPS), a machine-readable YAML specification that becomes the source of truth for every Data Product across all systems. We then walk through the full lifecycle of creating, updating, and managing Data Products through both catalog-based and pipeline-based workflows.

- Chapter 2 covers the G in Retrieval: governance. We define how to profile source systems before you connect to them, classify data at ingestion, enforce quality gates, automate metadata capture, track lineage, and manage retention and audit logging.

- Chapter 3 covers the A in Retrieval: architecture. We design a reusable pipeline template, make connector decisions, define orchestration and storage architecture, and build the monitoring and observability layer.

- Chapter 4 covers the P in Retrieval: people. We map existing roles to retrieval activities, define how to work with source system teams, and address training, descriptive metadata authoring, and incident response.

- Chapter 5 is a hands-on sample project that ties everything together. It takes a realistic scenario and implements what we designed in Chapters 1 through 4, using open-source tools so you can follow along without expensive vendor platforms.

There are a few things this book does not cover. We introduce the Open Data Product Standard (ODPS) but we do not cover the Open Data Contract Standard (ODCS). Data Contracts are a rich topic that deserves dedicated treatment, and we will cover them in depth in Volume 3 alongside the Integration and Value Extraction phases of DRIVE. Formal contracts between producers and consumers require a level of maturity that most source systems do not yet support. Volume 3 will pick up exactly where this book leaves off.

After reading this book, you will have a complete, implementable blueprint for the retrieval phase of any Data Product: from profiling a source system to having validated, classified, lineage-tracked data in a source-aligned Data Product, operated by a team that knows who does what and how to respond when things go wrong.

ONE

A Technical Definition of Data Products

Before we move into the technical aspects of Data Retrieval, we will first start with a technical definition of Data Products. Therefore, the first question we need to ask ourselves is, "Where does a Data Product exist?" With "exist," we do not mean only where the data is stored. We also mean where it is described and where it is consumed. This is a very tricky question, and most people will intuitively answer, "in the database."

While this might sound logical, it is not the full truth, because the database alone usually contains only the data itself, not the full product definition. A Data Product might also be represented in a data catalog, guarded through a data contract, implemented through pipelines in a Git repository and an orchestration tool, exposed through an API gateway, represented in a semantic layer or BI model, or offered through a dedicated data marketplace or portal.

Only physical data is usually stored in dedicated structures in data platforms, such as tables, files, or views. This means we need to think beyond storage and define a Data Product that spans multiple systems. We need a way to connect the product definition, its documentation, contracts, pipelines, and access mechanisms into a coherent whole. Different systems each contain part of the truth, and they must work together to consistently represent the same Data Product. At first glance, this can look like complex system integration, because it involves connecting multiple tools through interfaces and ensuring they stay aligned. Figure 2 highlights why this becomes complex quickly.

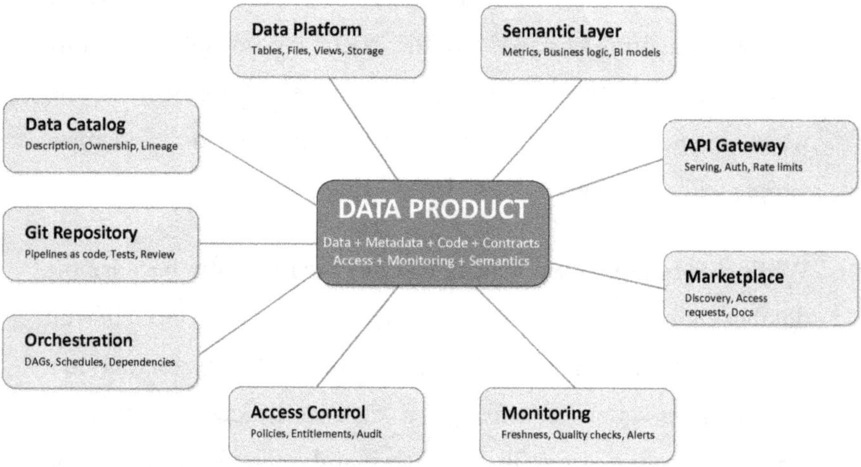

Figure 2: Data Product complexity.

Figure 2 shows that a Data Product exists across multiple systems and only works if these parts are connected. Simply storing data in a data platform is not enough. We also need versioned transformation logic in a Git repository, orchestration to run and manage dependencies, and a catalog that describes the product, its assets, and its lineage. We need access control and an API gateway to expose the product securely, and we need monitoring to ensure quality, freshness, and reliability over time. We also need a semantic layer so consumers understand metrics and business logic consistently. Since these elements live in different tools, we later need a common, standard description that ties them together into one coherent Data Product. The illustration shows the full set of building blocks, even though not every Data Product will implement every block from day one.

At first glance, this appears to be a pure integration issue. We have many systems, each holding part of the Data Product, and we need them to work together. The good news is that we can make this far easier by standardizing how we describe a Data Product across those systems. This is where industry standards come in.

We have two powerful standards that help us: one for Data Products and one for Data Contracts. Both are hosted under the Linux Foundation and are managed by Bitol.[1] They are called the Open Data Product Standard (ODPS) and the Open Data Contract Standard (ODCS). We will return to ODCS in Volume

[1] The Bitol Project: https://bitol.io/.

3. For now, we start with ODPS. Both standards use YAML as a practical representation format, which makes them easy to read, version, and share.

Creating a standardized document for a Data Product should be the first step when creating a new Data Product because it becomes the shared source of truth across all systems involved. It forces us to define ownership, purpose, interfaces, and expectations before implementation begins, preventing fragmented definitions across the catalog, pipelines, the semantic layer, and access. Because the document is machine-readable, it enables automation from day one, including generating catalog metadata, validating contracts, provisioning access, enforcing policies, and setting up monitoring and alerts. This is the very first step to proper DataOps because it turns Data Product delivery from manual coordination into a repeatable, automatable lifecycle.

Open Data Product Standard

Now let's start digging into the technology. We will first have a look at the schema of ODPS. Since standards evolve, you might want to check the current version of the standard in Bitol's Git repository: https://github.com/bitol-io/open-data-product-standard. The repository contains the schema, examples, and useful tools for working with the standard.

As a first step, let's look at the top-level elements of the standard:

```
apiVersion: v1.0.0
kind: DataProduct
status: active

id: 7c2f1a4e-9b3d-4e8a-a1c5-2f6d8e0b4a17
version: v2.1.9
name: Customer Churn Product
domain: Sales
tenant: The Data Product Company

description: ...

inputPorts: ...

outputPorts: ...

authoritativeDefinitions: ...

support: ...

team: ...

productCreatedTs: ...

tags: ...
```

This excerpt shows the core structure of the Open Data Product Standard in a compact form. The first block (apiVersion, kind, status) defines the Data Product's specification version, document type, and lifecycle status.

The next block (id, version, name, domain, tenant) identifies the Data Product and places it in its organizational context.

After that, ODPS uses nested sections that capture the substance of the product: the description explains the purpose and content; inputPorts and outputPorts define how the product consumes and exposes data; and authoritativeDefinitions, support, and team document definitions, responsibilities, and contact points.

Finally, fields like productCreatedTs and tags add lifecycle metadata and classification, which helps with discovery and governance. In the next sections, we will go through key elements in detail.

Let's start with the first block from the above definition:

Element	Description
apiVersion	Specifies which ODPS specification version the Data Product document follows. This is not the version of the Data Product itself, but the version of the ODPS standard used to structure and interpret the YAML.
kind	Defines the document type in ODPS. It is a fixed identifier that tells tools and readers that this YAML describes a Data Product entity, not another artifact. In the current standard, the only valid value is `DataProduct`, and it is also the default.
status	Expresses the current lifecycle state of the Data Product. It makes clear whether the product is still being prepared, already in use, or on its way out. The standard defines a fixed set of valid values: proposed, draft, active, deprecated, or retired. This field supports lifecycle management by making the maturity and availability of the Data Product explicit for consumers and platform processes.

Now let's focus on the Data Product-specific elements:

Element	Description
id	This is the unique identifier of the Data Product. It exists to avoid collisions when names change or when different products share similar names. It should be stable over time and is typically implemented as a UUID. Tools use it as the primary reference for linking the Data Product across systems.
version	The version of the Data Product itself, not the ODPS standard version. It tracks changes to the product over time. This field is optional and could also be derived from Git, for example from release tags or commit history.
name	This is the human-readable name of the Data Product. It should be clear and recognizable for consumers.
domain	This specifies the business domain the Data Product belongs to. It provides context and supports discovery and ownership by grouping products by domain. Typically, the name of the domain is derived from the business capabilities an organization has.
tenant	This identifies the organization the Data Product belongs to. It is mainly used to separate products across organizations or tenants in multi-tenant setups. While not mandatory, it might be useful in large multinational companies.

While the first elements are straightforward, we now have more complex elements. The first one is the "description," which provides more granular information about a Data Product for users.

```
description:
   purpose: Churn data for better ad targeting
   limitations: May only be used within the Sales
department.
   usage: Check input and output ports
```

The description block captures the essential context needed to understand and use the Data Product correctly. It documents the intended purpose, the recommended usage, and any limitations, including technical, compliance, or legal constraints. It can also reference authoritativeDefinitions to link to sources that provide deeper detail and formal definitions. If required, customProperties can be used to add structured key-value information specific to the organization.

Every Data Product needs incoming data. This can either be plain data or Data Products it builds on. This is defined as an inputPort. The inputPort defines what a Data Product expects from upstream data. A name and version identify it, and it references the agreed expectations via contractId, which links to the underlying data contract. We will have a look at Data Contracts in Volume 3 of this series. Tags and customProperties allow classification and organization-specific details. authoritativeDefinitions can be used to link to sources that explain the input in more depth. There must be at least one input Port for a Data Product but there can also be more. The following shows the key elements of an input port.

```
inputPorts:
 - name: Sales Data
   version: 1.2.0
   contractId: sa_mas_salesData
```

The outputPort mirrors the inputPort. An outputPort is what the Data Product exposes to the external world and in what form. A Data Product must expose at least one outputPort. It is identified by name and version and can include a short, human-readable description, along with a type indicating how the port is exposed and handled. If a contract exists for the output, it can be referenced via contractId and dependencies can be made explicit through inputContracts.

```
outputPorts:
 - name: Monthly Churn Data
   description: Churn Data calculated on the last
day
   type: API
   version: 1.0.0
   contractId: ca_mas_customerChurn
```

Like inputPorts and outputPorts, a managementPort is a core element of a Data Product. A managementPort defines how the Data Product is managed and operated, for example, for discoverability, observability, control, or dictionary-related information. It is identified by name and content and can include a short description of its purpose and usage. The managementPort can be exposed as a REST endpoint or a topic and accessed via a URL or a communication channel.

```
managementPorts:
 - content: discoverability
   type: rest
   name: dp-disc-api
   url:                                https://my-
company.internal/apis/churn/product
```

An authoritativeDefinition links the Data Product to a trusted source of truth. It combines a type that describes what kind of reference it is, and a URL that points to the actual source. Typical types include business definitions, implementation details, transformation logic, or tutorials. An optional description can clarify what the reader will find at the link.

```
authoritativeDefinitions:
  - type: Legal Definition
    url:                                          https://my-
company.internal/legal/dataproducts
```

A support block defines how consumers can get help for a Data Product. It is identified by a channel and a URL, for example, an email address, a Slack or Teams channel, or a ticketing page. The tool specifies which system is used, and the scope clarifies whether the channel is meant for interactive support, announcements, or issue handling.

```
support:
  - channel: support
    url: mailto:support@dataproduct.com
    tool: email
    scope: issues
```

The team block defines who is responsible for the Data Product. It can include a team name, a short description, and a list of members. The goal is to make ownership visible so consumers know who builds, operates, and maintains the product.

```
team:
   name: Sales Insights
   description: The Sales Insights Team within Sales
   members:
```

```
    - username: sandy.goats@dataproduct.com
      name: Sandy Goats
      description: Data Product Owner
      role: owner
```

Another composite element, though an easy one to use, is "tags". Tags are simple labels that can be attached to the Data Product or to individual elements, depending on where the field is placed. They help categorize and filter products, for example, by sensitivity, subject area, or internal classification.

```
tags: ['churn', 'customer', 'sales']
```

Now that we have the main Element defined, we need to start using it. Since it is YAML, you can basically integrate it into all your workflows. As mentioned in the beginning, the main place where a Data Product "lives" is within a Git repository. You would then automate everything from there (e.g., via GitHub Actions) and have the merges done from this location. This now requires several processes, which we will elaborate on in the next section.

Processes for Data Products

Creating a Data Product from scratch

Every Data Product starts with a need. Not a technical need, but a business need. Someone in the organization realizes that they need data they do not have, or that the data they have is unreliable, scattered, or simply not in a form they can work with. This is the moment where a Data Product is born, and we must handle it well from the very beginning.

The worst thing that can happen at this stage is that someone sends an email, makes a phone call, or walks over to the data team and says, "I need some data." This might sound harmless, but it is the beginning of chaos. Without a structured request, the data team does not know what is needed, who needs it, why it matters, or how urgent it is. The result is often a quick fix that turns into a permanent workaround, which is exactly the kind of data thinking we want to leave behind.

I learned this the hard way. In one organization, I was the service portal. People came to me directly with their data requests, sometimes by email, sometimes by chat, sometimes by grabbing me in the hallway. Everyone believed their request was the most urgent one. And when nothing got delivered fast enough, they asked why. The problem was not the team's capacity; it was the lack of process, prioritization, and transparency. Everyone was shouting into the void, and the void was me.

I quickly changed this by introducing a proper intake process and, more importantly, shifting the prioritization responsibility to the business units themselves. We used wallet sizing as the mechanism: each business unit received a fixed budget for Data Product requests, and they had to decide how to spend it. This changed the conversation entirely.

Instead of "Why is my request not done yet?" the question became, "Which of our requests delivers the most value?" That shift from entitlement to ownership made all the difference.

A single point of entry

To avoid the chaos of ad-hoc requests, every organization that takes Data Products seriously needs a single point of entry for requesting new Data Products. The good news is that most organizations already have service portals in place, whether it is ServiceNow, Jira Service Management, or a similar tool. We do not need to build a new portal from scratch. We need a dedicated service request type for Data Products within the existing portal. This keeps the barrier low for requesters, as they already know where to go and how the process works, while providing the data team with a structured, traceable intake channel.

Adding a Data Product request type to your existing service portal does several things at once. First, it creates a record. Every request is documented, timestamped, and traceable. Second, it forces the requester to think. By asking the right questions upfront, the request form helps the requester articulate what they need, rather than what they think they need. Third, it creates a queue. Requests can be prioritized, assigned, and tracked, preventing the data team from drowning in ad hoc requests that all claim to be urgent.

Now, the critical question is, "What should this service request collect?" This is where many organizations go wrong. They either ask too little, which means the data team must chase missing information, or they ask too much, which means nobody wants to fill out the form. We need a balance. The goal is to collect just enough information to evaluate the request, estimate the effort, and decide, without turning the intake form into a bureaucratic nightmare.

Here are the essential fields that a Data Product request should capture. These are the minimum fields needed to move forward. Everything else can be clarified in follow-up conversations once the request has been accepted:

- **Requester name and department**. Who is requesting the Data Product and from which business unit? This establishes accountability and helps with prioritization. Sample: *Anna Schmidt, Marketing.*

- **Business purpose.** A short description of why this Data Product is needed and what business question it should answer. This is the most important field because it defines the "why." Sample: *"We need to understand customer churn patterns to improve retention campaigns."*

- **Estimated business impact**. The expected value that this Data Product will deliver. This can be monetary or strategic. We discussed in Volume 1 how to assess the business impact of Data Products, and this is where that thinking becomes practical. Even a rough estimate helps enormously with prioritization and with the financial evaluation that follows. Sample: *"Reducing churn by 2% would save approximately €1.5M annually."*

- **Expected consumers**. Who will use this Data Product? This can be individuals, teams, or systems. Knowing the consumers early shapes how we design access and output ports. Sample: *Marketing Analytics team, Campaign Management system.*

- **Known data sources**. Which systems or datasets does the requester believe contain the relevant data? This does not need to be precise, but it gives the data team a starting point. Sample: *CRM system, billing platform, customer support tickets.*

- **Freshness requirement**. How current does the data need to be? This determines whether we need real-time, near-real-time, or batch processing, which has a major impact on architecture and cost. Sample: *Daily refresh is sufficient.*

- **Expected timeline**. When does the requester need the Data Product? This helps with prioritization and resource planning. Sample: *Q3 this year.*

- **Sensitivity and compliance**. Does the data involve personal information, financial data, or other regulated content? This triggers governance and security requirements early. Sample: *Contains personal customer data, GDPR applies.*

- **Sponsor or budget owner**. Who is funding this Data Product? This is important because Data Products require ongoing maintenance, and someone needs to own the cost beyond the initial build. Sample: *VP Marketing.*

Notice that we are not asking for technical details like table structures, transformation logic, or specific tools. That is by design. The requester is typically a business user, and we do not want to burden them with decisions that belong to the data team. The request captures the what and the why, while the how comes later.

From request to evaluation

Once a request arrives, it does not automatically become a Data Product. It enters an evaluation phase. This is where the data team, ideally in collaboration with a Data Product Owner or a domain steward, reviews the request and decides whether to proceed. Not every request should become a Data Product. Sometimes the data already exists in another product. Sometimes the effort is disproportionate to the value. Sometimes the requester needs a one-off analysis, not a product.

The evaluation should answer a few key questions. First, "Does a similar Data Product already exist?" One of the biggest sources of waste in data organizations is building products that overlap with existing ones. If there is already a Customer 360 Data Product, and the new request wants "a complete view of our customers," we should extend the existing product rather than building a new one. This is where a data catalog becomes essential, because it allows the team to check what already exists before committing to new work.

Second, "Are the data sources available and accessible?" A request might sound reasonable, but if the underlying systems do not expose data in a usable way, the effort to retrieve it might be massive. This is not a reason to reject the request, but it must be factored into the estimation. Third, "Is there a clear consumer with a real use case?" If the requester cannot identify who will use the Data Product and for what purpose, the request is likely premature. We build Data Products for consumers, not for completeness. Fourth, "Is there a budget and sponsorship?" Data Products are not free. They require development, infrastructure, and ongoing maintenance. If nobody is willing to fund it, the product will become an orphan the moment the initial excitement fades.

This evaluation should not take weeks. A lightweight review, perhaps a 30-minute conversation between the requester and the data team, is usually enough to decide whether to proceed, park, or reject the request. The outcome is a simple decision: proceed to the next phase, defer, or decline. If the decision is to proceed, the request moves into the design phase, where we assess the business case before we commit to building anything.

Designing the Data Product

Before we jump into technical definitions and YAML files, there is a step that many data teams skip, and it costs them dearly later. Once the initial evaluation gives the green light, the request must pass through a financial gate. This is where controlling or finance evaluates the estimated business impact and aligns it with organizational priorities and available budget.

This might sound like unnecessary overhead, but it is the opposite. It protects both the data team and the business. Without a financial evaluation, we risk building Data Products that nobody is willing to pay for once the initial enthusiasm wears off. We also risk investing months of engineering effort into something that delivers marginal value compared to other requests in the queue.

The design phase is about answering one fundamental question: "Is the expected business impact worth the investment?" The estimated impact from the service request is a starting point, but it needs validation. Controlling or finance should review the numbers, challenge assumptions, and compare the expected return against the cost of building and maintaining the Data Product. This does not require a full business case document. A structured conversation between the requester, the Data Product Owner, and a finance representative is usually sufficient.

What makes this step different from the evaluation before it is the audience and the depth. The evaluation checks feasibility: "Can we build it?" The design phase checks viability: "Should we build it?"

These are fundamentally different questions, and they involve different stakeholders.

The design phase also serves as an alignment mechanism. It ensures that the requester's expectations match what the data team can realistically deliver within the given budget and timeline. If the estimated impact is $1.5 million in annual savings, but the build cost is $2 million, that is a conversation that needs to happen before anyone writes a single line of code.

The outcome of the design phase is a confirmed go/no-go decision, supported by financial alignment and stakeholder commitment. Only when this gate is passed do we move into defining the Data Product technically. This might feel like it slows things down, but in practice, it accelerates delivery by preventing wasted effort on products that lack organizational support.

Defining the Data Product

This is where we bridge the gap between business need and technical implementation. The first concrete technical artifact we produce is the Data Product definition using the Open Data Product Standard we discussed earlier in this chapter. This might sound formal, but it is the single most important step in the entire process, because it turns a validated business case into a structured, machine-readable specification.

The Data Product Owner, usually someone from the domain team, works with the data team to complete the ODPS YAML. At this stage, not every field needs to be complete. But the essential sections must be defined: the name, domain, description, purpose, expected input ports, and at least a preliminary output port. The team section should also be populated to make ownership clear from day one.

Why is this step so important? Because the ODPS YAML becomes the source of truth for everything that follows. It is what gets committed to Git. It is what triggers automation. It is what the catalog reads. It is what the monitoring checks against. If we skip this step or treat it as optional, we lose the ability to manage the Data Product as a coherent whole across systems. We are back to scattered definitions, undocumented pipelines, and invisible ownership, which is exactly what we wanted to avoid. Once the ODPS YAML is drafted, it gets committed to a Git repository. This is the moment when the Data Product officially becomes a managed entity. From here, everything can be automated and tracked. Don't worry about ODPS much; most, if not all, will be generated from the information collected in the earlier steps.

Setting up the infrastructure

With the Data Product defined in ODPS and committed to Git, the technical setup begins. This typically involves several steps that can run in parallel, depending on the organization's platform maturity.

First, the pipeline scaffolding is created. Based on the input ports defined in the ODPS YAML, the data engineering team sets up the initial retrieval pipelines. We will go deep into retrieval in the following chapters, so we will not cover the technical details here. What matters at this point is that the pipeline structure reflects the product definition, not the other way around. The ODPS YAML drives the implementation, not a random script someone wrote.

Second, the data contracts are referenced. If the Data Product consumes data from upstream systems or other Data Products, the expectations for those inputs should be formalized. Data Contracts are a rich and important topic that deserves dedicated treatment, so we will cover them in depth in Volume 3 of this series. For now, what matters is that the Data Product's input ports clearly state what they expect, and that these expectations are documented and agreed upon with upstream providers.

Third, the catalog entry is created. The Data Product must be registered in the organization's data catalog to become discoverable. This can be automated from the ODPS YAML, a key benefit of using a standardized format. The catalog entry should reflect the current status, for example, "in development," so that potential consumers know the product exists but is not yet ready for use.

Fourth, access control and security are configured. Based on the sensitivity and compliance fields in the initial request, the appropriate access controls are configured. This includes defining who can read the data, who can modify the product, and whether encryption, masking, or anonymization is required. Getting this right early avoids painful retrofitting later, especially when personal data or regulated information is involved.

Fifth, monitoring and alerting are initialized. Even before the first data flows through the product, the monitoring framework should be in place. This includes freshness checks, schema validation, volume anomaly detection, and quality rules. The monitoring should be built into the product, not bolted on as an afterthought. If we wait until the product is in production to add monitoring, we will always be one step behind when issues occur.

Building and going live

Once the infrastructure is in place, the actual development work begins. Pipelines are built and tested, transformations are implemented, and the output ports are validated against the expected specifications. This is also where the Medallion architecture typically comes into play: data moves from Bronze to Silver to Gold, with quality and structure increasing at each level. One important thing to note here, as discussed in Volume 1, is that we might have a smaller scope per data product, so the typical medallion might not be fully leveraged.

Before the Data Product goes live, it should pass through a readiness check. This does not need to be a heavy governance gate, but it should verify a few essentials.

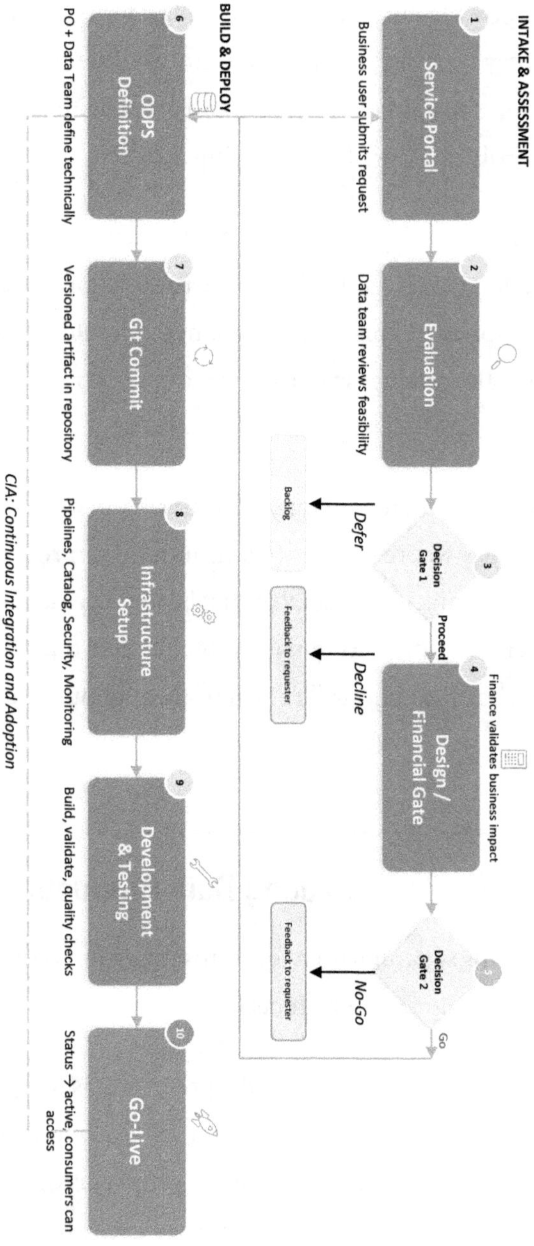

Figure 3: Data Product processes.

Is the data flowing correctly? Are the quality rules passing? Is the catalog entry complete and accurate? Is the documentation sufficient for consumers to understand and use the product? Are access controls in place? Is monitoring active?

If the readiness check passes, the Data Product status in the ODPS YAML is changed to "active," and the product becomes available for consumption. This status change should automatically propagate to the catalog, so consumers can discover and access the product.

And this is where many organizations think the work is done. It is not. This is where CIA (Continuous Improvement and Adaptation) begins. The Data Product is now alive and needs care, feedback, and iteration to remain valuable. But that is a topic we covered in the recap and will return to throughout this book.

Common pitfalls in creating Data Products

Let us close this section with a few traps that teams commonly fall into when creating Data Products from scratch.

The first pitfall is skipping the intake process. It is tempting to just start building, especially when a senior stakeholder asks for something urgently. But without a proper request, we lose traceability, we cannot prioritize, and we often build the wrong thing. The intake form takes five minutes, while rebuilding a misunderstood Data Product takes months.

The second pitfall is skipping the financial gate. Enthusiasm is not a business case.

If we do not validate the expected business impact before we start building, we risk delivering a product that nobody is willing to fund in the long term. The design phase exists to prevent expensive regret.

The third pitfall is over-engineering the first version. A Data Product does not need to be perfect at launch. It needs to be correct, documented, and useful. Start with the most critical output port and the most important consumers and expand from there. Trying to cover every possible use case in version one is a guaranteed way to delay delivery and frustrate stakeholders.

The fourth pitfall is treating the ODPS definition as paperwork. If the team sees the YAML as a bureaucratic exercise rather than a functional specification, it will be incomplete and out of date within weeks. The ODPS YAML must be a living artifact that drives automation and reflects reality. If it does not, it becomes just another document that nobody trusts.

Catalog-based updates of a Data Product

A Data Product does not stop changing after it goes live. Business contexts shift, teams get reorganized, new regulations apply, and the way people describe and classify data evolves over time. Most of these changes have nothing to do with pipelines or transformation logic. There are changes to the metadata, the documentation, and the organizational context around the Data Product. And the place where these changes happen most naturally is the data catalog.

The catalog is the shop window of your Data Products. It is where business users go to discover what exists, understand what a Data Product contains, and decide whether they can trust it. For most consumers, the catalog is the only touchpoint they have with a Data Product. They never see the pipelines, the YAML files, or the Git repository.

This is why catalog-based updates matter. They are essential for keeping Data Products trustworthy and discoverable over time.

What gets updated via the catalog

Not every change to a Data Product should happen through the catalog. Technical changes to schemas, pipelines, or transformation logic belong in a different workflow, which we will cover in the next section. But there is a broad set of changes that is best handled through the catalog because they originate on the business side, not on the engineering side.

The most common catalog-based updates include changes to descriptions and purpose statements. When the business context shifts, the way we describe a Data Product needs to shift with it. A product that was originally built for "ad targeting" might evolve to also support "customer retention analysis." If the description does not reflect this, potential consumers will not find it or will misunderstand its scope.

Tags and classifications are another frequent update. As new use cases emerge or organizational taxonomies evolve, the labels attached to a Data Product need to be adjusted. A product tagged only as "marketing" might also become relevant to "customer service" or "product development." Tags are the primary mechanism for filtering and discovering Data Products, so keeping them up to date directly affects adoption.

Ownership and team changes happen more often than we like to admit. People leave the organization, teams get restructured, and responsibilities shift. When the team section of a Data Product definition still lists someone who left six months ago, consumers do not know who to contact when something goes wrong.

Support channel updates follow a similar pattern. Slack channels get renamed, ticketing systems get replaced, and email distribution lists change. If the support information in the catalog points to a dead channel, consumers are left without a path to get help.

Sensitivity and compliance labels may need updating as regulations change or as the Data Product begins consuming new data sources with different restrictions. A product that initially contained no personal data might expand its input ports to include customer identifiers, which changes its compliance profile entirely.

Finally, documentation links need maintenance. Tutorials are rewritten, business glossaries are moved to new platforms, and authoritative definitions are updated. If the links in the catalog still point to outdated or broken resources, the Data Product becomes harder to use correctly.

The sync problem

Here is where things get tricky. We established earlier in this chapter that the ODPS YAML in Git is the source of truth for a Data Product. Everything flows from that definition: the catalog entry, the monitoring, the access controls. But now we are saying that people should be able to update descriptions, tags, and ownership through the catalog UI. That creates a tension. If someone changes a description in the catalog, but the ODPS YAML in Git still contains the old text, which one is correct?

This is the central technical challenge of catalog-based updates, and if we do not solve it, we end up with two competing sources of truth. The catalog says one thing, Git says another, and nobody knows which one to trust. We have seen this problem in many organizations, and it always ends the same way: people stop trusting both.

There are different ways to solve this. Some organizations treat Git as the absolute master and make the catalog entirely read-only, meaning every change must go through Git directly. This is clean from a technical perspective, but it creates a high barrier for business users who are not comfortable with Git workflows. Other organizations allow bidirectional sync, where both the catalog and Git can initiate changes, but this introduces complexity and the risk of merge conflicts that are hard to resolve automatically.

The approach I recommend sits in the middle: the catalog serves as the user-friendly interface for changes, but each change is pushed to Git via a pull request. This keeps Git as the single source of truth while allowing non-technical users to make changes through the catalog UI they already know. The flow works like this: a user edits a field in the catalog, the catalog system automatically creates a pull request in the Git repository with the corresponding change to the ODPS YAML, a reviewer approves the pull request, the merge updates the ODPS YAML, and the updated YAML propagates back to all connected systems, including the catalog itself.

This approach has several advantages. It keeps Git as the authoritative source, so there is never ambiguity about what the current truth is. It provides an audit trail through Git history, so every change is traceable. It introduces a review step, which catches errors before they propagate. And it works with the tools business users already use, because they interact with the catalog, not with Git directly.

The key technical prerequisite is that the catalog must support this kind of integration. Not every catalog tool does this out of the box, but modern data catalogs increasingly offer Git integrations or webhook capabilities that enable this workflow. When evaluating catalog tools, this should be a key selection criterion.

Who should be allowed to update what?

Not every field in a Data Product definition should be editable by everyone. Allowing unrestricted changes through the catalog is a recipe for inconsistency and accidental damage. We need role-based permissions that reflect the different responsibilities people have in relation to a Data Product.

The following table shows a practical permission model for catalog-based updates. It distinguishes between three roles: business users who consume or interact with the Data Product, Data Product Owners who are accountable for the product, and the data engineering team who builds and maintains the technical infrastructure.

Field	Business user	Data Product Owner	Data engineering team
Description and purpose	Can suggest (via review)	Can edit	Can edit
Tags and classifications	Can suggest (via review)	Can edit	Can edit
Owner and team members	No	Can edit	No
Support channels	No	Can edit	Can edit
Sensitivity and compliance labels	No	Can edit	No

Field	Business user	Data Product Owner	Data engineering team
Documentation links	Can suggest (via review)	Can edit	Can edit
Status (lifecycle)	No	Can edit	No
Input and output ports	No	No	Can edit
Schema and technical details	No	No	Can edit
Contracts and SLAs	No	No	Can edit

A few things are worth noting here. Business users can suggest changes to descriptions, tags, and documentation, but those suggestions go through a review process, which is the pull request we described earlier. They should not be able to modify these fields directly, as unreviewed changes can introduce inconsistencies.

Data Product Owners have the broadest editing rights for business-facing fields. They are the ones accountable for how the product is described, classified, and governed. They are also the only ones who can change ownership or lifecycle status, as these decisions carry organizational consequences.

The data engineering team controls everything technical: ports, schemas, contracts, and SLAs. These fields should never be editable through the catalog because changes to them require technical validation and testing. They belong in the pipeline-based update workflow.

This separation might seem rigid, but it prevents a common problem: well-meaning people making changes that break things downstream. This is exactly why business users cannot edit sensitivity labels: an update made without understanding the technical implications could accidentally remove access controls. And it is why ownership changes are reserved for the Data Product Owner: a team lead who changes the owner field during a reorganization might break alerting chains.

The silent killer: Catalog rot

There is one more problem we need to address, and it is perhaps the most dangerous one because it happens slowly and invisibly. Catalog rot is what happens when nobody maintains catalog entries over time, such as:

- Descriptions become outdated.
- Tags no longer reflect reality.
- Documentation links break.
- Owner fields list people who left the company a year ago.

The insidious thing about catalog rot is that it does not cause an immediate failure. The data still flows. The pipelines still run. The dashboards still update. But consumers gradually lose trust in the catalog. They start asking colleagues instead, or they build their own shadow catalogs in spreadsheets. And once consumers stop trusting the catalog, discoverability collapses. New Data Products go unnoticed. Existing ones get duplicated because people do not know they already exist. We are back to the chaos we wanted to avoid.

The antidote is a combination of ownership and automation. On the ownership side, Data Product Owners must treat catalog maintenance as part of their ongoing responsibility, not as a one-time task during the initial setup. This should be part of the CIA cycle we introduced in Volume 1.

On the automation side, the platform can help by detecting staleness. Simple checks can go a long way: flag Data Products whose descriptions have not been reviewed in six months, alert when a team member listed in the owner field is no longer active in the organization's identity system, highlight documentation links that return 404 errors, or surface Data Products whose tags have not changed since creation despite the product evolving through multiple versions.

These automated checks should not create busywork. They should surface meaningful signals that help Data Product Owners keep their products healthy. Think of it as a routine health check for your Data Products. You do not wait until something breaks. You inspect, maintain, and update proactively.

Connection to ODPS

One benefit of using the Open Data Product Standard is that catalog-based updates are not just free-text edits. They map to specific, structured fields in the ODPS YAML. When someone updates a description in the catalog, that change corresponds to the description.purpose field in the standard. When someone adds a tag, it maps to the tags array. When someone updates a support channel, it maps to the support block.

This structure makes validation possible. The platform can check whether a change is well-formed before it creates a pull request. It can enforce that certain fields are not left empty. It can verify that a new sensitivity label is one of the allowed values in the organization's taxonomy. This is a significant advantage over catalogs that treat metadata as unstructured text, because it means catalog-based updates are not just documented but also validated and consistent.

It also means that the catalog UI can be generated from the ODPS schema. Instead of designing a custom form for every catalog, we can use the standard to drive the interface: show the right fields, enforce the right constraints, and automatically map every change back to the YAML. This reduces implementation effort and ensures that the catalog stays aligned with the standard as it evolves.

Pipeline-based updates of a Data Product

In the previous section, we looked at updates that change how a Data Product is described. Now we look at updates that change how it works. Pipeline-based updates are changes to the technical substance of a Data Product, including schemas, transformation logic, data sources, quality rules, and output ports. These changes always originate from engineering, never from the catalog UI, and they always start in Git.

If catalog-based updates are about keeping the shop window accurate, pipeline-based updates are about changing the engine under the hood. And just like with a real engine, changes here can have consequences that ripple far beyond the component you touched.

What triggers a pipeline-based update?

Pipeline-based updates do not happen on a schedule. They happen because something changes, either in the environment or in the requirements. The most common triggers are:

- **A new or changed data source**. An upstream system gets migrated, a new source becomes available, or an existing source changes its format or delivery mechanism. This requires changes to the input ports and the retrieval logic of the Data Product.

- **Schema evolution**. New fields need to be added, existing fields need to change their data types, or deprecated columns need to be removed. Schema changes are among the most impactful updates because they affect everything downstream.

- **Changed business rules**. A KPI gets redefined, a calculation changes, or a new aggregation is required.

This means the transformation logic inside the Data Product needs to be updated, typically at the Silver or Gold layer of the Medallion architecture.

- **Bug fixes**. A join was incorrect, a filter excluded records it should not have, or a data type conversion caused silent data loss. These are urgent changes that need to be deployed quickly but carefully.

- **New or modified output ports.** A new consumer needs data in a different format, with different granularity, or delivered via a different mechanism. This changes what the Data Product exposes to the outside world.

- **Quality rule adjustments**. Thresholds that were initially set too loosely or too tightly need recalibration, or entirely new quality checks need to be added based on production experience.

Not all of these triggers carry the same risk. Adding a new optional field to an output port is fundamentally different from changing the data type of an existing column. This is why we need to think carefully about the impact of each change before we deploy it.

The impact radius

This is where pipeline-based updates become dangerous if handled carelessly. Unlike catalog updates, which are largely cosmetic, pipeline changes can break downstream consumers.

Changing a schema, modifying a transformation, or removing an output field can cascade through dependent Data Products, dashboards, APIs, and machine learning models that rely on the affected output.

Before any pipeline change is merged, the team must understand its impact radius. Who consumes this Data Product? Which fields do they use? Which downstream Data Products are built on top of it? This is where lineage becomes essential. A lineage tool, or lineage information in the data catalog, can show the dependency graph and make visible which consumers and products are affected by a given change. Also, Data Contracts and clear YAML definitions help here, as they describe who is using it.

The impact radius determines how the change should be handled. A low-impact change, like adding a new optional field, can usually be deployed without coordination. A high-impact change, like renaming or removing a field that downstream consumers rely on, requires communication, planning, and possibly a deprecation period before the change goes live. We will cover this in more detail when we discuss versioning below.

The following table provides a practical overview of common pipeline changes, their typical impact, and how they should be handled:

Change type	Impact	Example	Recommended approach
New optional field added	Low	Adding a "last_login_date" column to an output port	Deploy directly, update documentation
Performance optimization	Low	Changing partitioning strategy or query tuning	Deploy after testing, transparent to consumers
New quality rule added	Low	Adding a freshness check on an input port	Deploy directly, monitor for false positives
Bug fix (data correction)	Medium	Fixing an incorrect join that excluded valid records	Deploy, communicate to consumers, consider backfill
New data source added	Medium	Adding a new input port from a previously unused system	Deploy after validation, update ODPS YAML
Transformation logic changed	Medium to High	Recalculating a KPI due to changed business rules	Coordinate with consumers, validate output against expectations
Field data type changed	High	Changing a column from string to integer	Deprecation period, parallel versions, consumer migration
Field removed or renamed	High	Removing a column that downstream products depend on	Deprecation period, consumer communication, staged rollout
Output port restructured	High	Changing the granularity or format of an entire output	Treat as new version, run old and new in parallel

The key takeaway is simple: the higher the impact, the more coordination is needed before deployment. Low-impact changes can flow through the standard deployment pipeline. High-impact changes require explicit alignment with consumers before anything changes in production.

The deployment flow

Every pipeline-based update follows the same basic flow, regardless of its impact level. The process starts in Git and ends with the updated Data Product running in production and all connected systems reflecting the change. A developer creates a feature branch and makes the necessary changes to the pipeline code and, if applicable, to the ODPS YAML. Normally, changes to ODPS should be automated. We could add decorators (e.g., in Python) to pipelines that add this kind of information. Both live in the same repository, which ensures that the technical implementation and the product definition stay in sync. The developer then opens a pull request.

The pull request triggers automated checks. These include schema validation, unit tests for transformation logic, and data quality tests that run against a staging or development environment. The depth of testing depends on the impact level of the change. A low-impact change might only need basic validation. A high-impact change should include regression tests that compare the output before and after the change to ensure nothing unexpected has shifted.

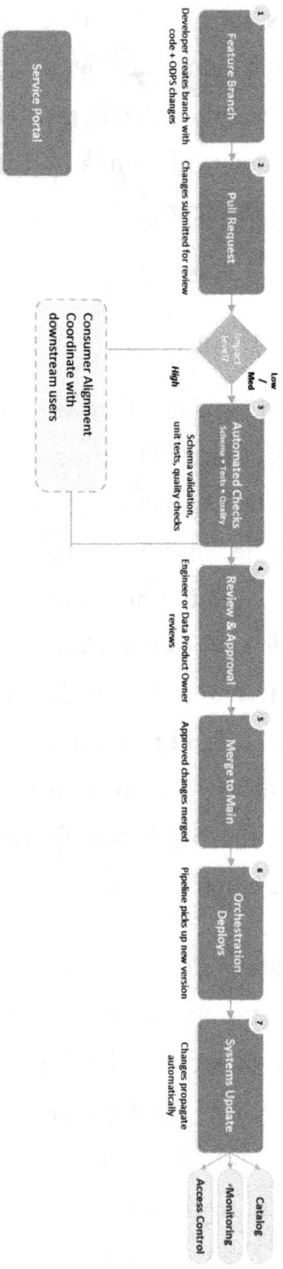

Figure 4: The deployment flow.

A reviewer, typically another engineer or the Data Product Owner for high-impact changes, reviews the pull request. The review checks both the technical correctness and the alignment with the product definition. If the ODPS YAML was updated, the reviewer also verifies that the changes are consistent with the business intent.

Once approved, the pull request is merged into the main branch. From here, the orchestration system picks up the new version and deploys it. This can be fully automated for low-impact changes or require a manual approval gate for high-impact changes, depending on the organization's risk appetite.

After deployment, the changes propagate to all connected systems. The catalog is updated to reflect the new schema or output port. Monitoring adjusts to the new quality rules or thresholds. Access controls are reconfigured if the sensitivity profile changes. This propagation is automated through the ODPS YAML, which is why maintaining it as a living artifact is so important.

Key learnings

- **A Data Product spans multiple systems**: It is not just a table in a database. It spans the Git repository, data catalog, orchestrator, API gateway, semantic layer, and monitoring stack. Only by connecting these pieces through a shared standard does a Data Product become a coherent whole.

- **ODPS turns product definitions into automation**: The Open Data Product Standard gives us a machine-readable, versionable YAML that drives everything downstream: catalog entries, pipeline scaffolding, monitoring, and access control.

- **Every Data Product starts with a need, not a pipeline**: A structured creation process from service request through financial evaluation to ODPS definition and infrastructure setup prevents the chaos of ad-hoc requests.

- **Catalog-based and pipeline-based updates serve different purposes**: Metadata and documentation changes flow through the catalog with Git-backed pull requests. Technical changes to schemas, transformations, and quality rules flow through Git directly.

Two

The G in Retrieval

In Volume 1, we established that governance is not a separate discipline bolted onto Data Products after the fact. It is embedded into every step of the DRIVE framework, starting with retrieval. We also made a conscious decision: we do not use the term "data governance" in conversation, because it carries baggage. Too many organizations have tried and failed with governance programs that were disproportionate, over-engineered, and never made it beyond PowerPoint slides. Instead, we take quality for granted. We talk about building high-quality Data Products, and governance becomes the mechanism that makes this possible.

In the retrieval phase, specifically, Volume 1 introduced several foundational ideas. We learned that data quality starts before retrieval even begins, at the point where data is entered into source systems. We introduced Data Contracts as agreements between producers and consumers that define what data is delivered, in what format, and under what conditions. We outlined the four types of metadata that should be captured from the very beginning: descriptive, technical, administrative, and structural. And we acknowledged that managing upstream dependencies through DAGs is essential for reliable retrieval.

All of that was intentionally kept at a conceptual level. We explained what needs to happen and why it matters. Now, in Volume 2, we go deeper. This chapter explains how to implement governance in the retrieval phase. Not as theory, but as practical, repeatable engineering work that you can apply to your own Data Products.

We will walk through the full governance lifecycle of data retrieval, from profiling source systems before you connect to them, through classifying and quality-checking data as it arrives, to automatically capturing metadata, tracking lineage, managing retention, and logging everything for compliance. Each section builds on the previous one, and by the end of this chapter, you will have a concrete governance framework for the retrieval phase that you can implement in your organization.

One important boundary: this chapter focuses exclusively on governance. We will not discuss architecture or people here, even though they are equally important parts of the GAP triad. Those dimensions get their own dedicated chapters later. And we will stay within the retrieval phase. Governance for integration and value extraction follows in subsequent parts of the book.

Let us start where every retrieval should start: by understanding what we are connecting to.

The starting point: source system profiling

When we start from scratch, a Data Product begins with a connection to a source system. This holds true for every source-aligned Data Product.

This sounds straightforward, but it is one of the most consequential decisions in the entire lifecycle. The moment we connect a pipeline to a source, we inherit everything that source entails: its quality issues, its schema quirks, its downtime patterns, and its compliance obligations. If we do not understand what we are connecting to, we are building on a foundation we cannot trust.

Source system profiling is the governance practice of assessing a source system before it becomes an input port for a Data Product. It is the inspection you do before you buy the car, not after you have already driven it off the lot.

Why profile before you connect?

In many organizations, the process of connecting to a new source system looks like this: someone on the data team receives a request, gets database credentials or an API endpoint, writes an ingestion script, and data starts flowing. It works. Everyone is happy. Until it does not work anymore.

The problems usually surface weeks or months later. The schema changes without warning and the pipeline breaks. Null values appear in fields that were never null before. Data volumes spike during month-end processing and the pipeline times out. A column that looked like an integer turns out to contain text in edge cases that only appear in certain regions. The source system goes down for maintenance every Sunday night, exactly when the batch job is scheduled.

None of these are rare events. The question is not whether they will happen, but whether we are prepared for them when they do. Profiling is how we prepare.

There are three reasons why profiling before connecting is non-negotiable for Data Products.

The first reason is quality protection. A Data Product without quality does not deliver value. We established this principle in Volume 1, and it starts here. If we do not know the quality baseline of a source system, we cannot set meaningful quality gates on our input ports. We would be guessing at thresholds, and guessing at quality is the same as not managing it at all. Profiling gives us the facts: how complete the data is, how consistent the formats are, how many duplicates exist, and how stable these numbers are over time.

The second reason is risk management. Not every source system is equally safe to connect to. Some contain highly regulated personal data. Some are legacy systems running on infrastructure that could be decommissioned next year. Some are owned by teams that have no interest in supporting downstream consumers. Connecting to these sources without understanding the risks means we might build a Data Product that violates compliance requirements, depends on a system that will not exist in twelve months, or breaks repeatedly because the source team keeps changing things without telling us. Profiling makes these risks visible before we commit engineering effort.

The third reason is cost avoidance. Building a retrieval pipeline is not free. It takes engineering time, infrastructure resources, and ongoing maintenance. If we connect to a source that turns out to be unusable, we waste all of that investment. Worse, we waste the time of the consumers who were waiting for the Data Product. I have seen teams spend weeks building pipelines to source systems that turned out to deliver data so inconsistent that the entire ingestion had to be redesigned from scratch. A two-hour profiling exercise at the beginning would have surfaced these issues before a single line of pipeline code was written.

When a company acquires another company, due diligence checks are done. For a Data Product, this is the due diligence we need to ensure the Data Product keeps its promise.

The seven dimensions of a source system profile

A source system profile should cover seven dimensions. These are not arbitrary. They map directly to the governance concerns that affect whether a source can reliably feed a Data Product. Each dimension answers a specific question that the data team needs answered before they commit to building a connection.

The first dimension is the data quality baseline. This answers the question, "How clean is the data today?" Before we can define quality gates on our input ports, we need to know what the source actually delivers. This means measuring null rates across key fields, checking for duplicate records, validating format consistency, and identifying outliers or anomalies.

A practical approach is to request a sample extract from the source system and run a profiling tool against it. Tools like Great Expectations, Soda, or even basic SQL queries can surface the key quality metrics within minutes. What matters is that the results are documented, because they become the baseline against which all future quality checks are measured.

The second dimension is schema stability. This answers the questions, "How often does the source system's schema change, and how are changes communicated?" Some source systems have formal release cycles where schema changes are announced weeks in advance. Others are managed by teams that add, rename, or remove columns without telling anyone. The difference between these two scenarios has a massive impact on how robust our retrieval pipeline needs to be.

During profiling, we should find out when the last schema change occurred, how it was communicated, and whether there is a documented process for schema evolution. If the source team has no change management process, we need to build defensive mechanisms into our pipeline, such as schema validation on every run. We should also understand the source system's release cadence: "Is it continuous deployment, quarterly releases, or ad-hoc changes?" This can't be solved with tools; it requires rigorous discussions with the source system teams.

The third dimension is volume and growth patterns. This answers the questions, "How much data are we dealing with, and how will it grow?" Volume affects everything from infrastructure sizing to cost estimation to pipeline design. A source that delivers 1,000 records per day requires a fundamentally different approach than one that delivers 10 million. While the first is low-hanging fruit for delivery, the latter is a complex engineering discipline that might require us to build a Kafka system.

Equally important are the patterns. "Does volume spike at certain times?" Month-end, quarter-end, holiday seasons, and campaign periods can all cause volume surges that a pipeline designed for average load cannot handle. Profiling should capture not just the current volume but also the growth trajectory and any known seasonality.

The fourth dimension is freshness and availability. This answers the question, "How current is the data, and when is it available for retrieval?" Some source systems update in real time. Others run batch processes overnight and only have complete data available by 6 AM. Some have maintenance windows where the system is completely unavailable.

Understanding freshness and availability is critical because it determines our retrieval strategy. If the source only has fresh data at 6 AM but our consumers need it by 7 AM, we have a one-hour window for the entire retrieval and processing pipeline. If the source has a four-hour maintenance window every Sunday, our pipeline needs to handle that gracefully. These constraints must be known upfront, as they lead to many design decisions we need to make.

The fifth dimension is technical accessibility. This answers the question, "What interfaces does the source system offer for data extraction?" The options vary widely. Some systems offer robust APIs with pagination and filtering. Others only support database replication or file exports. Some support Change Data Capture through transaction logs, while others only allow full table scans. And others are really difficult to access, as the source systems might be in a legacy database with legacy code such as COBOL. All my nightmares started with COBOL.

The available interface directly determines which retrieval pattern we can use: real-time streaming, CDC-based delta loads, timestamp-based deltas, or full loads. If the only option is a nightly

CSV export to an SFTP server, that constrains the entire architecture. Profiling should document all available interfaces, their limitations, and any known performance impacts on the source system during extraction.

The sixth dimension is ownership and contact. This answers the questions, "Who is responsible for this source system, and who do we contact when something goes wrong?" This might seem obvious, but in large organizations it is often surprisingly unclear. Source systems may be maintained by teams in different countries, managed by external vendors, or owned by business units that do not consider downstream data consumers part of their responsibilities. In fact, most of the companies I worked with just "stored" the data, without any reliable structure.

During profiling, we should identify the technical owner, the business owner, and the operational support contact. We should also understand the source team's willingness and capacity to support data consumers. A source system whose team actively communicates changes and responds to issues is a fundamentally different proposition from one whose team treats data extraction as someone else's problem.

The seventh dimension is the compliance profile. This answers the question, "What regulatory or legal constraints apply to the data in this source system?" If the source contains personal data, GDPR or other privacy regulations apply. If it contains financial data, there may be audit requirements. If it contains health data, there are sector-specific regulations to consider.

The compliance profile determines which governance controls must be in place before the first record is retrieved. It affects data classification, access controls, retention policies, and audit logging requirements.

The source system scorecard

Profiling is only useful if the results are captured in a structured, comparable format. This is why I recommend using a source system scorecard: a standardized document that summarizes the profiling results across all seven dimensions we just discussed and produces an overall readiness assessment.

The following table shows a practical scorecard format you can use in your company. Each dimension is scored on a scale from 1 to 10, where 1 means high risk or poor readiness and 10 means low risk or excellent readiness. The scores are not meant to be scientific. They are informed judgments by the data team based on the profiling exercise. If you want to be on the safe side, use the Delphi method we discussed in Volume 1.

Dimension	Key question	Score (1-10)	Notes
Data quality baseline	How clean is the data today?		Null rates, duplicates, format consistency
Schema stability	How often and how predictably does the schema change?		Change frequency, communication process

Dimension	Key question	Score (1-10)	Notes
Volume and growth	How much data, and how will it grow?		Current volume, growth rate, seasonality
Freshness and availability	When is fresh data available for retrieval?		Update frequency, maintenance windows
Technical accessibility	What extraction interfaces are available?		APIs, CDC, file export, replication
Ownership and contact	Who owns it and who supports it?		Technical owner, business owner, responsiveness
Compliance profile	What regulatory constraints apply?		PII, financial data, sector regulations

I strongly recommend storing this scorecard either in the Data Catalog or in the repository you use for your Data Product. This way, you can keep track of the product and update it if you realize the assumptions were wrong. Ideally, you store them in JSON or YAML for better machine and AI readability.

Classifying data at ingestion

Data that enters a Data Product without a classification label is data we cannot govern. We do not know who should be allowed to see it, how long we should keep it, whether it needs encryption, or whether special compliance rules apply. The longer the data sits unclassified, the harder it becomes to retroactively apply the right controls, because by then it may already have been copied, transformed, or exposed downstream.

In practice, unclassified data gets one of two treatments, and both are bad. Either it receives the most restrictive controls by default, which slows down everyone who needs to work with it. Or it receives no controls at all, which creates compliance risk that nobody is aware of until an audit or a breach forces the conversation.

Classification at the point of ingestion is the only approach that scales.

It ensures that governance controls are applied from the first moment data enters the Data Product, not retrofitted weeks later when someone remembers to check.

Classification schemas for data

A classification scheme for Data Products does not need to be complex. Four levels are sufficient for most organizations. What matters is that each level has clear criteria and clear consequences.

Organizations that already have a classification scheme should use it rather than inventing a new one for Data Products. The important thing is not the specific labels but that the scheme is applied consistently and that every classification level maps to concrete, enforceable governance actions.

Level	Criteria	Governance consequences
Public	Data that can be shared externally without restriction. No business sensitivity.	No access restrictions, standard retention, no encryption required
Internal	Data intended for internal use only. Business-relevant but not regulated.	Access limited to authenticated and known employees, standard retention
Confidential	Data containing personal information, financial details, or business-critical content.	Role-based access, encryption at rest and in transit, audit logging required
Restricted	Highly sensitive data subject to strict regulatory requirements (e.g., health data, credit scoring).	Named-person access only, full encryption, mandatory audit trail, specific retention mandated by regulation

Automating classification at the point of ingestion

Manual classification does not scale. If we rely on someone reviewing every dataset and assigning a label by hand, classification will be inconsistent at best and forgotten at worst. The goal is to automate as much of the classification as possible and only require human judgment for genuine edge cases.

Two practical approaches work well in combination.

The first is inheritance from the source system profile. This is the simplest and most reliable method. During source system profiling, we already assessed the compliance profile of the source. If we know that the CRM system contains personal customer data, every dataset retrieved from that system should automatically inherit a baseline classification of Confidential. This rule is defined once, attached to the source profile, and applied to every ingestion run. It requires no per-record analysis and correctly covers the majority of cases.

The second is pattern-based detection. This catches sensitive data that might not be obvious from the source profile alone. Pattern detection scans incoming data for known sensitive formats, such as email addresses, phone numbers, national identification numbers, credit card numbers, tax identifiers, and similar patterns. When a match is found, the classification is automatically elevated. For example, a dataset from an internal reporting system profiled as "Internal" might be reclassified to "Confidential" if pattern detection finds email addresses in one of the columns.

Pattern-based detection is not perfect. It produces false positives, for example, flagging a random number sequence as a potential credit card number, and it can miss sensitive data in unexpected formats. But it provides a valuable safety net that catches cases where the source profile alone would have underclassified the data. With Pattern-based detection, we need a human in the loop. This requires manual work, but it is more efficient than doing it fully manually, and only edge cases need to be handled manually.

When implementing automated classification, the results should be stored as metadata alongside the ingested data. This means that every record, or at a minimum every batch, carries its classification label from the moment it lands in the Bronze layer. Downstream processes can then read this label and apply the appropriate governance controls without needing to reclassify.

Data quality gates in data retrieval

Profiling told us what to expect from a source system. Classification told us how sensitive the data is. Now we need a mechanism to enforce our expectations at the boundary of the Data Product. This is what quality gates do. They sit at the input port and decide, for every ingestion run, whether the incoming data is good enough to enter the Data Product.

It is important to emphasize that quality gates at input ports are one-sided. We define what we expect, and we check what we receive. This is not a data contract, where both the producer and consumer agree on terms. In most enterprise environments, source systems do not support contracts. The CRM team will not sign an agreement regarding null rates in their export. The ERP system does not take our freshness requirements into account. This is the reality of data retrieval, and quality gates are our response to it. We cannot control what the source sends us, but we can control what we allow into our Data Product. Please note one thing here: ideally, we would start enforcing data contracts at data retrieval. This is possible for new systems, but for existing ones, which are often legacy, it might not be feasible.

The three decisions a quality gate makes

Every quality gate produces one of three outcomes for each ingestion run.

Accept means the data passed all checks and flows into the Data Product as expected. This is the normal case and should represent most ingestion runs. If gates are triggering constantly, either the source is unreliable or the thresholds are miscalibrated. It means we need to talk to the system owners and improve if feasible.

Flag means the data passed into the Data Product, but one or more checks raised a warning. The ingestion continues, but an alert is created so the data team can investigate. Flags are used for situations where blocking the data would be worse than letting slightly imperfect data through, for example, when a non-critical field has a higher null rate than usual but the core data is intact.

Reject means the data failed a critical check and is blocked from entering the Data Product. Rejected data does not disappear. It is sent to a quarantine zone for inspection, correction, and reprocessing. We will cover the quarantine pattern later in this section.

Defining quality rules for input ports

Quality rules define what "good enough" means for a specific input port. They should be concrete, measurable, and derived from the source system profile we created earlier. There are five rule types that cover the most important quality dimensions at ingestion.

Rule type	What it checks	Example
Completeness	Null values in fields that should not be null	Customer ID must not be null in more than 0.5% of records.
Validity	Values conform to expected format, type, or range	Order date must be a valid date, not in the future.
Uniqueness	No unexpected duplicates on key fields	Order ID must be unique within each batch.
Freshness	Data is recent enough to be useful	Most recent record timestamp must be within 24 hours of ingestion time.
Volume	Row count is within expected range	Batch must contain between 800 and 12,000 records (based on historical pattern).

Not every rule type applies to every input port. A low-volume reference data source might only need completeness and validity checks. A high-volume transactional source might need all five. The source system profile provides the baseline for deciding which rules matter and what thresholds to set. This also shows clearly why the first step of profiling is so important here!

Hard gates versus soft gates

Not all quality rules carry the same weight. Some violations are critical and must stop the pipeline. Others are concerning but not worth blocking an entire ingestion run. This distinction is captured in the difference between hard gates and soft gates.

A hard gate stops the pipeline when a rule fails. No data enters the Data Product until the issue is resolved. Hard gates are appropriate for rules where allowing bad data through would cause serious downstream damage: a missing key, a corrupted schema, or a batch that contains zero records when thousands were expected. Hard gates protect the Data Product from garbage that would be painful or impossible to clean up after the fact.

A soft gate lets data through but raises an alert. Soft gates are appropriate for rules where the violation is worth knowing about but not worth blocking the entire ingestion. A slightly elevated null rate on a non-critical field, or a minor deviation from expected volume, might warrant investigation but should not prevent the Data Product from receiving its daily refresh.

Beyond hard and soft, there is an important question of granularity: "Does a failure affect the entire batch or individual records?" Modern data platforms like Databricks explicitly support this distinction. A "fail all" strategy rejects the entire batch if any rule fails. This is the safest approach but also the most disruptive, because one bad record can block thousands of good ones. A "fail row" strategy rejects only the individual records that violate the rule and lets the rest pass through. This is more granular and less disruptive, but it requires the pipeline to handle partial batches and route rejected rows to quarantine separately.

The right choice depends on the rule type and the data. For schema-level violations, fail all is usually the only option because the entire batch is structurally compromised. For record-level violations, such as a null value in a specific field, a fail row is often the better choice because it preserves the majority of the data while isolating the problem.

A practical starting point is to use hard gates with fail all for structural checks (schema validation, batch not empty) and soft gates or hard gates with fail row for record-level checks (completeness, validity, uniqueness). This gives maximum protection against structural failures while maintaining pragmatism for individual data quality issues. One thing is important here: when we fail all or rows alone, we need to react fast. When all fail, business users will immediately see it: "There is no data". With a failed row, business users will see data, but it might be incomplete and decisions are based on partly correct data.

The quarantine pattern

Rejected data needs somewhere to go. If we simply discard it, we lose the ability to understand what went wrong, to fix the data, and to reprocess it. This is why every quality gate setup needs a quarantine zone.

A quarantine zone is a dedicated storage area, separate from the main Data Product layers, where rejected data is stored along with the rejection reason. The quarantine zone serves three purposes. First, it enables investigation. The data team can inspect rejected records, identify the root cause, and determine whether the issue lies in the source, the pipeline, or the quality rules themselves. Second, it enables reprocessing. Once the issue is resolved, whether by fixing the data or adjusting the rules, the quarantined records can be reprocessed and flow into the Data Product as if they had passed the gate originally. Third, it provides evidence. Quarantine records create a trail of what was rejected and why, which is valuable for conversations with source system teams to improve data quality upstream.

The quarantine zone should be treated as a temporary holding area, not a permanent archive. Records should either be reprocessed into the Data Product or deleted after a defined retention period. A quarantine zone that grows indefinitely is a sign that underlying quality problems are not being addressed.

In my experience, these quality gates were simple "If/Else" statements, with no audit trail or lineage. Finding issues in the data was challenging, as someone needed to dig deep into the SQL queries or pipelines. Modern data platforms support a complex analysis of this and help identify the root cause.

Calibrating thresholds from your source profile

The most common mistake in setting up quality gates is using arbitrary thresholds. Setting a null rate threshold at 1% because it "feels right" is not governance. Thresholds must be calibrated against the source system profile we created in the first section of this chapter.

If profiling showed that a source system consistently delivers a 3% null rate on a particular field, setting the gate at 1% guarantees constant failures. Setting it at 3% means every minor fluctuation triggers a rejection. A reasonable approach is to add headroom above the observed baseline: set the threshold at 4%, which is tight enough to catch genuine degradation but loose enough to absorb normal variation. Also, it makes sense to group them, for instance: flag 1-4%, and reject 4% and above.

This calibration should be revisited periodically. Source systems change over time, and what was a normal baseline six months ago might no longer reflect reality. Quality gate thresholds should be part of the CIA cycle we discussed earlier, reviewed and adjusted based on production experience. Also, it is important here to work with the source system team to gradually improve their data quality. The desired state is that they finally apply data contracts. (We will introduce data contracts in detail in Volume 3.)

Operationalizing quality gates

Quality gates are only useful if they run reliably, report clearly, and alert the right people. In practice, gates should be implemented as a dedicated step in the ingestion pipeline, running after data lands in a staging area but before it enters the Bronze layer of the Data Product. This ensures that no unvalidated data reaches the Data Product's main storage.

Gate results should be logged for every ingestion run: which rules were evaluated, the measured values, and the outcome (accept, flag, or reject). These logs feed into the Data Product's monitoring dashboard and become part of the audit trail we will discuss later in this chapter.

Alerts should be targeted. A hard gate failure that blocks ingestion should notify the data engineering team immediately, as the Data Product will not receive fresh data until the issue is resolved. A soft gate flag can go to a monitoring channel for review during business hours.

Automating metadata capture

In Volume 1, we introduced four metadata types to be collected from the very beginning: descriptive, technical, administrative, and structural. We explained why each type matters and what happens when metadata is missing. But we left the how for this book.

In most organizations, metadata collection looks like this: someone builds an ingestion pipeline, the data starts flowing, and weeks later, someone remembers that the new source should probably be documented. A wiki page gets created. It includes column descriptions, a link to the source system, and a timestamp that will never be updated. Within months, the documentation is outdated and nobody trusts it.

This approach does not work for Data Products. Metadata cannot be a manual afterthought. Every ingestion run should automatically emit metadata alongside the data it delivers. The pipeline writes two things: the data to the Bronze layer, and a metadata record to the catalog or a metadata store. If the pipeline ran, the metadata is current.

The good news is that three of the four metadata types from Volume 1 can be largely automated at the retrieval layer. One cannot.

What to capture at every ingestion run

The following table maps each of the four metadata types to what can be captured automatically during retrieval and what still requires human effort.

Metadata type	Automated at retrieval?	What the pipeline captures
Technical	Fully	Schema snapshot (columns, data types, nullable), file format, compression, encoding, source system identifier, row count, file size, ingestion timestamp.
Administrative	Mostly	Source system owner (from source profile), classification label (from the classification step), access constraints (from ODPS definition). Legal constraints and usage conditions still need human input at setup, but should be in ODPS.

Metadata type	Automated at retrieval?	What the pipeline captures
Structural	Partially	Pipeline dependency graph (from DAG definition), input port references (from ODPS). Cross-product relationships and broader data model context need human input but can also be profiled from software.
Descriptive	Minimal	Column names are captured automatically. Business descriptions, glossary terms, and the kind of clarity we described in Volume 1 with the "fname" example require human authoring. However, this only needs to be done once for the setup.

Implementing capture in the pipeline

In practice, automated metadata capture works as a sidecar step in the ingestion pipeline. After data lands in the staging area and passes through the quality gates we discussed in the previous section, the pipeline emits a metadata record that captures the essential facts about this specific ingestion run.

A metadata record should include the source system identifier, the pipeline ID and version, the run timestamp, a schema snapshot, the row count, the quality gate results, and the classification label that was applied. This single record connects everything we have built so far in this chapter: the source profile tells us where the data came from, the classification tells us how sensitive it is, the quality gate results tell us whether it passed inspection, and the schema snapshot tells us exactly what structure arrived.

Schema snapshots deserve particular attention. By capturing the full schema at every ingestion run, we can automatically detect schema drift. If today's schema differs from yesterday's, that is a signal worth investigating immediately. A new column might indicate an upstream release that nobody communicated. A changed data type might break downstream transformations. A removed column may result in data loss. None of these requires manual monitoring if the pipeline automatically captures the schema and compares it with the previous run. This ties directly back to the schema stability dimension we assessed in the source system profile.

The metadata record should be pushed to the data catalog via API, making it immediately visible and searchable for anyone who needs to understand the Data Product. Additionally, a copy of the schema snapshot could be versioned in Git alongside the ODPS YAML, so that schema evolution is traceable through the same version history that tracks everything else about the Data Product.

For organizations using orchestration tools such as Airflow or Dagster, much of this metadata is already available in the run context. The task is not to generate new information but to capture what the pipeline already knows and route it to the right destination. This is an engineering task that is solved once per pipeline template and then reused across all Data Products.

What automation cannot solve

We need to be honest about what automation cannot do. Descriptive metadata, the business meaning of fields, glossary terms, KPI definitions, and usage guidance cannot be generated by a pipeline. No amount of automation will turn a column named "fname" into a clear description of what the field contains, how it should be interpreted, and what its business context is. That is human work, and it must be done by people who understand the domain.

Lineage from source to landing zone

Lineage answers two questions: "Where did this data come from, and how did it get here?" In a full Data Product lifecycle, lineage spans the entire journey from source system through Bronze, Silver, and Gold to the output port. But at the retrieval layer, we scope it tightly. We track lineage from the source system to the landing zone, meaning the Bronze layer. What happens after that belongs to the integration phase and will be covered in Volume 3 of this series. Even this narrow slice is valuable. When a quality gate flags a problem, lineage tells us which source system delivered the bad data and which pipeline moved it. When a consumer questions a number, lineage provides the first link in the chain of evidence. And when a source system announces a schema change, lineage tells us which Data Products are affected.

Table-level versus column-level lineage

Lineage can be tracked at different levels of granularity, and the choice has significant implications for cost and usefulness.

Table-level lineage tracks which source table fed which pipeline and landed in which target table. It answers questions like "this Bronze table was loaded from the CRM system's orders table via pipeline X at 03:15 this morning." This level of granularity is relatively cheap to implement because the information is already available in the pipeline definition and the DAG. It covers the majority of debugging and impact analysis scenarios at the retrieval layer.

Column-level lineage tracks which specific source column maps to which specific target column. It answers more precise questions, such as "the customer_email column in the Bronze table came from the email_addr column in the CRM system." This is significantly more expensive to implement and maintain because it requires parsing the transformation logic and keeping the mapping up to date as schemas evolve.

The practical recommendation is to start with table-level lineage for all Data Products and add column-level lineage selectively only when genuinely needed. Two scenarios justify the additional investment. The first is regulated data classified as Confidential or Restricted. When auditors ask "where does this personal data come from and where does it go," column-level lineage provides the precise answer that table-level lineage cannot. The second is impact analysis for volatile source systems. If a source system that scored low on schema stability in the source profile changes a column, column-level lineage tells us exactly which downstream fields are affected, rather than just flagging that "something in this table might have changed."

For everything else, table-level lineage at the retrieval layer provides sufficient visibility at a fraction of the cost.

Capturing lineage automatically

The good news is that most of the information needed for retrieval-layer lineage already exists in the artifacts we have built throughout this chapter. The DAG definition specifies which pipelines run in which order. The ODPS YAML knows which input ports connect to which source systems. The metadata sidecar from the previous section already captures the source system identifier, pipeline ID, run timestamp, and schema snapshot.

Lineage capture at the retrieval layer is therefore not about building a new system. It is about connecting these existing pieces into a coherent graph. A lineage record for a single ingestion run should contain the source system and source table, the pipeline that executed the retrieval, the run timestamp, the target location in the Bronze layer, and the row count. For column-level lineage, it also includes the column mapping between the source and target.

These records are pushed to the data catalog, which most modern catalog tools can render as a visual lineage graph. They are also stored as part of the audit trail we will discuss in the final section of this chapter.

Using lineage when things go wrong

Lineage proves its value in two concrete scenarios that every data team will encounter.

The first is debugging. When a quality gate rejects a batch or flags an anomaly, the immediate question is, "Where did this data come from?" Without lineage, the answer involves checking pipeline logs, asking colleagues, and tracing connections manually. With lineage, the answer is one query away: source system X, table Y, pipeline Z, ingested at timestamp T.

The second is impact analysis. When a source system announces a change, whether a schema modification, a decommission, or a migration, the data team needs to know which Data Products are affected. Lineage provides this answer directly. Combined with the schema snapshots from the metadata capture step, lineage can even show exactly which fields are at risk. This is the foundation for the pipeline-based update process we described in Chapter 1: before any change is deployed, lineage tells us who will be impacted.

Retention, compliance, and audit logging

Not all data has the same lifecycle. Some data is actively used in daily processing and must be available instantly. Other data is only needed if we have to reprocess a historical batch. And some data has served its purpose entirely and should be deleted. A tiered retention model reflects these differences.

The following table maps the classification levels we defined earlier in this chapter. Note that these are not recommendations, just samples. They need to be tailored to your organizational requirements and applicable laws:

Classification	Hot (active storage)	Warm (archive, accessible)	Cold (deep archive)	Delete
Public	90 days	1 year	Not needed	After warm
Internal	90 days	1 year	3 years	After cold
Confidential	180 days	2 years	5 years	Per regulation
Restricted	Per regulation	Per regulation	Per regulation	Per regulation

The pattern is straightforward: the more sensitive the data, the more retention is driven by regulation rather than by operational convenience. For Restricted data, every retention decision must be traceable to a specific legal requirement.

When law says keep versus when law says delete

Retention gets complicated when two legal obligations collide. GDPR and similar privacy regulations give individuals the right to have their data deleted. Financial sector regulations in many jurisdictions require companies to retain transaction records for seven to ten years. Healthcare regulations have their own mandates. When a single dataset contains both personal data subject to deletion rights and financial records subject to retention mandates, the data team is caught between two legal requirements.

Rather than treating an entire dataset as a single retention unit, retention rules should apply at the field or record level, where possible. Personal identifiers can be anonymized or deleted while the transactional data they were attached to is retained in anonymized form. This is not trivial to implement, but it is the only approach that satisfies both obligations simultaneously. When in doubt, legal counsel or the Data Protection Officer must be involved, and the decision must be documented as part of the Data Product's governance record.

Retention as policy-as-code

Retention policies that exist only in policy documents do not get enforced. Someone has to remember to run the cleanup, and in practice, nobody does.

The solution is to define retention rules as code that executes automatically. Retention policies should live alongside the ODPS

YAML in the Git repository, normally as a dedicated policy file. They specify the retention tier for each classification level, the transition rules between tiers, and the deletion or anonymization logic for data that reaches the end of its lifecycle.

An automated retention job runs on a schedule, evaluates each dataset against its policy, and executes the appropriate action: move to warm storage, move to cold archive, anonymize, or delete. Every action is logged, creating a record that proves the policy was enforced.

The key principle is that no manual intervention should be required for routine retention management. The policy is defined once, versioned in Git, and enforced automatically. Exceptions, such as a legal hold that suspends deletion for a specific dataset during an investigation, should be explicit overrides that are also tracked and documented.

The audit trail

The topics discussed in this chapter, including profiling, classification, quality gates, metadata capture, lineage, and now retention, produce actions that need to be provable.

Every ingestion run should produce an immutable audit record that captures the source system and table, the pipeline and its version, the run timestamp, the row count, the quality gate results (accept, flag, or reject), the classification label applied, the lineage reference, and any retention actions executed. This record is append-only. It cannot be modified or deleted, because its purpose is to provide evidence that governance controls were applied as defined. The audit record structure is simple. It does not need to capture the data itself, only the facts about what happened to the data. A single line per ingestion run, stored in a dedicated audit log that is separate from operational pipeline logs.

Making it all queryable

An audit trail that exists but cannot be searched is useless when an auditor asks a question. The goal is to answer any question about "what happened to this data" within minutes. This means the audit log must be stored in a queryable format, whether that is a simple database table, a structured log in a search platform, or a dedicated audit store. Auditors should be able to filter by source system, Data Product, time range, classification level, or quality gate outcome. When an auditor requests, "Show me all ingestion runs for Confidential data in the last quarter that had quality gate flags," the answer should be a single query, not a week-long investigation through scattered log files.

Audit logs also have their own retention requirements. In regulated industries, audit records often need to be retained longer than the data they describe. This should be defined as part of the retention policy-as-code, ensuring that audit log lifecycle management is automated alongside everything else. With the audit trail in place, we close the governance loop for the retrieval phase. Each step builds on the previous one, and together they form a practical, implementable governance framework for the first phase of any Data Product.

Key learnings

- **Profile before you connect**: The seven dimensions of the source system scorecard are due diligence for every Data Product. A two-hour profiling exercise prevents weeks of rework later.

- **Classify at ingestion, not retroactively**: Four classification levels with concrete governance consequences for each. Automated classification through source profile inheritance and pattern-based detection scales. Manual classification does not.

- **Quality gates enforce expectations at the boundary**: Hard gates stop critical violations, soft gates flag concerns without blocking. Calibrate thresholds based on the source system profile, not on gut feeling. And always have a quarantine zone because rejected data that disappears is data you cannot learn from.

- **Three of the four metadata types can be automated and should be emitted as a pipeline sidecar on every ingestion run**: Descriptive metadata requires human authoring and must be captured early, not retrofitted.

THREE

The A in Retrieval

In Volume 1, we covered the essential retrieval patterns. We learned when to use streaming and when batch processing makes more sense. We explored three approaches to Change Data Capture: the outbox pattern for systems we control, Write-Ahead Logs for databases we can listen to, and trigger-based CDC as a last resort. We walked through batch strategies from file-based loading to timestamp-based deltas to full loads, and we understood why full loads should remain the exception. We introduced DAGs as the mechanism for managing dependencies between retrieval steps, and we listed tools like Airbyte, Debezium, Airflow, and Dagster without explaining how they work together.

In Chapter 2, we defined the governance rules that must apply during retrieval: profiling sources before connecting, classifying data at ingestion, enforcing quality gates at input ports, automatically capturing metadata, tracking lineage, managing retention, and logging everything for compliance.

What we have not done yet is connect the two. The patterns from Volume 1 tell us how to move data. The governance rules in Chapter 2 specify the controls that must be in place. This chapter designs the architecture that brings both together into a coherent, repeatable infrastructure. We will define the blueprint for a retrieval pipeline that every Data Product in your organization can use, from extraction through validation to the source-aligned Data Product that stores the result. This chapter stays at the architectural level. We make design decisions and explain their trade-offs, but we do not configure tools or write pipeline code. That is the job of the sample project later in this book, where we will implement what we design here. The following image shows how the Data Product architecture is built. This is deliberately different from a "classical" data architecture diagram since we see Data Products as a moving thing. This volume of the book focuses on the retrieval part; the entire architecture will be extended to consumer-aligned, aggregated products in the next volume.

The internals of the retrieval pipeline

Every retrieval pipeline, regardless of the source system or the extraction pattern, follows the same fundamental structure. Understanding this structure is critical because it serves as the reusable blueprint for every Data Product in your organization. Rather than designing a new pipeline from scratch for each Data Product, we design the architecture once and parameterize it for each product. The ODPS is our starting point for this.

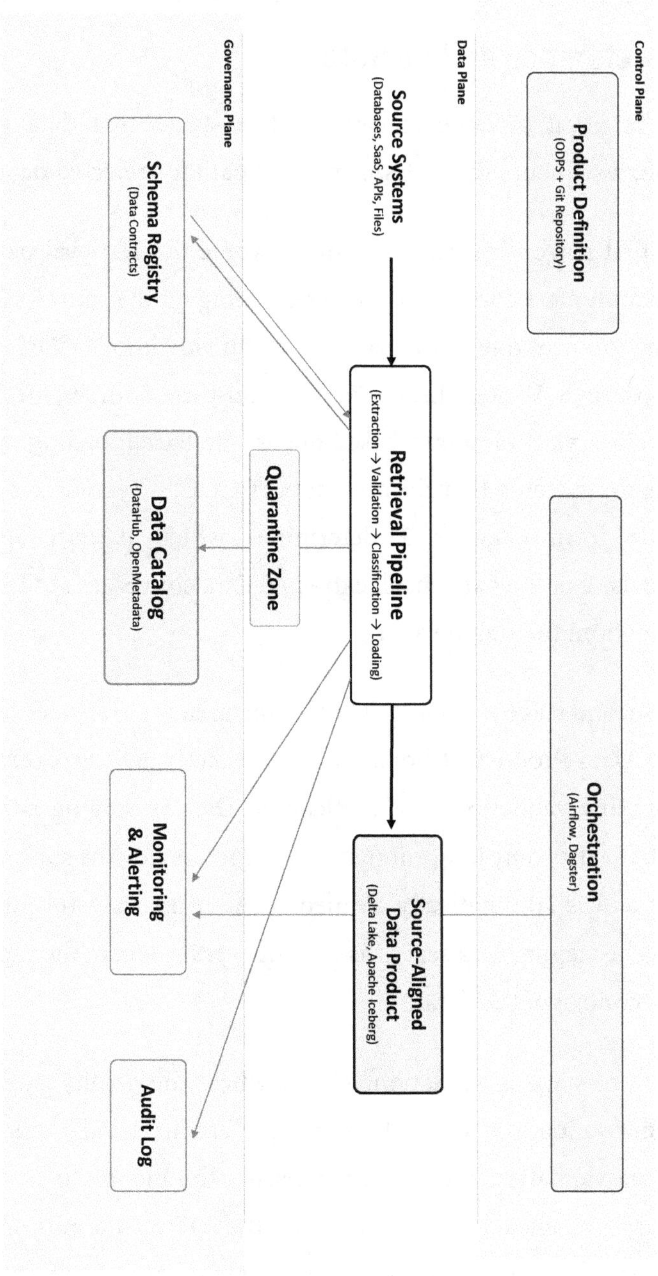

Figure 5: Building the Data Product architecture.

The reference architecture

The retrieval pipeline consists of five stages that data passes through sequentially, with one parallel path for rejected data.

The first stage is extraction. This is where the retrieval patterns from Volume 1 come into play. Depending on the source system, extraction uses one of the patterns we already know: CDC via an outbox or a Write-Ahead Log for real-time sources, or batch extraction via timestamp-based deltas, file-based loading, or full loads for systems that do not support CDC. The source system profile from Chapter 2 determines which pattern applies. Regardless of the pattern, all extracted data converges at the same destination: the staging area.

The second stage is staging. The staging area is a transient buffer, not a Data Product. It holds raw data exactly as it was received, before any validation or classification. Data in staging is short-lived. It exists only long enough to be processed by the subsequent steps and is automatically cleaned up after a successful pipeline run. The staging area serves as the entry point where the pipeline takes control of the data.

The third stage is validation. This is where the quality gates and schema validation from Chapter 2 are architecturally enforced. Schema validation runs first, comparing the incoming structure against the expected schema from the ODPS definition, and validates from a schema registry. If the schema is structurally compromised, the entire batch is rejected. If the schema passes, the data quality rules execute: completeness, validity, uniqueness, freshness, and volume checks. Each rule is configured as either a hard gate or a soft gate, with fail-all or fail-row granularity as we defined in Chapter 2. The validation stage produces one of two outcomes for each record or batch: accept or reject.

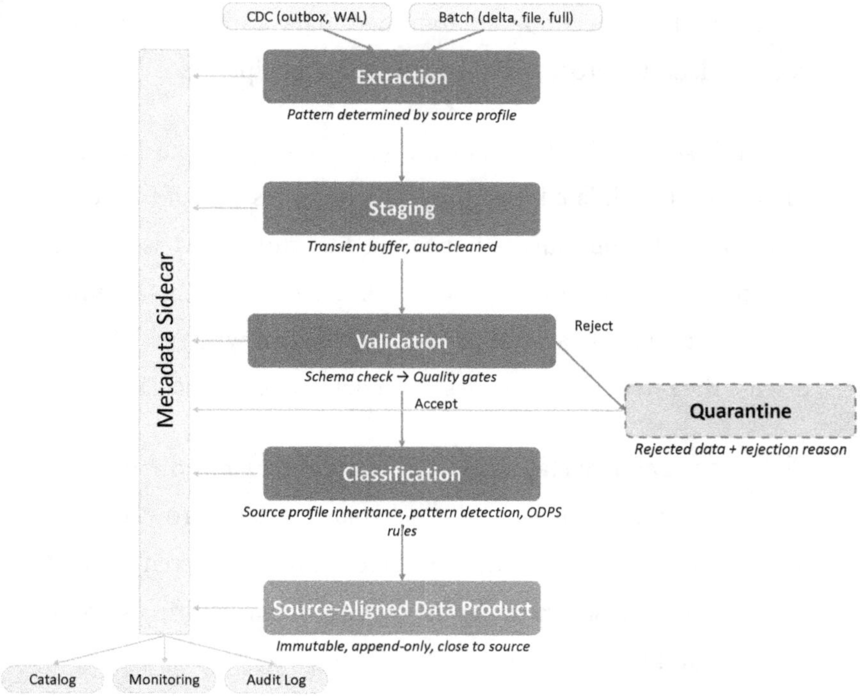

Figure 6: Five stages of the retrieval pipeline.

Accepted data moves to the fourth stage: classification. The classification labels from Chapter 2 are applied here, using the layered approach we described: source profile inheritance as the baseline, pattern-based detection as a safety net, and ODPS-driven rules for product-specific requirements. The classification label is attached as metadata and travels with the data from this point forward.

Rejected data follows a parallel path to the quarantine zone. The quarantine stores rejected records, along with the rejection reason, the quality rule that triggered the failure, and the pipeline run that produced the rejection. Quarantined data can be inspected, corrected, and reprocessed through the same pipeline.

The fifth stage is loading into the source-aligned Data Product. This is where validated, classified data becomes part of the actual Data Product. The source-aligned product stores data as close as possible to how the source delivered it, with minimal transformation. Data is appended, never overwritten. We will discuss the physical storage design in detail later in this chapter.

Throughout all five stages and the quarantine path, the pipeline emits a metadata sidecar: the schema snapshot, row counts, quality gate results, classification labels, lineage references, and timestamps. This sidecar feeds the catalog, the monitoring system, and the audit log, as we designed in Chapter 2.

One template, many Data Products

The architecture described above is not specific to a single Data Product. It is a template. The extraction pattern, quality rules, classification level, target location, and schedule are all parameters that differ per Data Product. Depending on what data platform you use, you would provide this as a template that is reused in this platform (e.g., Databricks or Snowflake).

This means that when a new Data Product is created through the process we described in Chapter 1, the data engineering team does not build a new pipeline from scratch. They configure an instance of the template by pointing it to the right source, applying the right quality rules, and setting the right schedule. The architecture stays the same; only the parameters change.

This is the foundation for DataOps in the context of Data Products: a repeatable, automated, and consistent pipeline architecture that scales with the number of products without proportionally increasing the engineering effort. Every Data Product that follows this template automatically inherits the governance controls from Chapter 2, because those controls are built into the architecture itself, not applied as an afterthought.

How to decide what connectors to use

In the pipeline anatomy we just described, extraction is the first stage. It is also the stage with the most architectural variation, because the right extraction approach depends entirely on what the source system supports. Volume 1 covered the retrieval patterns themselves: CDC via outbox, Write-Ahead Log, or triggers for real-time sources, and batch strategies like timestamp-based deltas, file-based loading, or full loads for everything else.

What we did not cover is how to choose the right tooling to implement those patterns. That is what this section addresses.

The goal is not to recommend a specific tool. Tools change, ecosystems evolve, and what is the best choice today might be replaced in two years. Instead, we define a decision framework that helps you select the appropriate connector category for each source, based on the source system profile we learned about in Chapter 2.

What connectors exist?

Connector tooling falls into three broad categories, each suited to different extraction patterns and source system characteristics.

The first category is managed or pre-built connectors. These tools provide ready-made connectors for common source systems, including databases, SaaS applications, cloud services, and file systems. You configure a connection, define the sync schedule, and the tool handles extraction, schema detection, and incremental loading. Airbyte and dlt are well-known open-source options in this space. Fivetran is a widely used commercial alternative. The strengths of managed connectors are the speed of setup and the breadth of coverage. If your source is a standard system like Salesforce, PostgreSQL, or Google Analytics, a pre-built connector will get you running in hours rather than weeks. The limitation is flexibility. When a source has non-standard behavior, unusual authentication, or a proprietary API, pre-built connectors may not cover the edge cases. Especially Airbyte has a strong ecosystem but not every connector is equally stable.

The second category is CDC frameworks. These are specialized tools designed for capturing changes from database transaction logs in real time. Debezium is the dominant open-source option, typically paired with Apache Kafka as the event bus. Kafka Connect provides the integration layer that moves change events from the database log into the streaming infrastructure. CDC frameworks are the right choice when you need real-time or near-real-time data propagation and the source database supports log-based change capture. They implement the Write-Ahead Log pattern we described in Volume 1. The strength is low latency and minimal impact on the source system. The limitation is operational complexity. Running a CDC framework requires managing a streaming infrastructure, which is a significant architectural commitment.

The third category is custom extraction. This covers everything that pre-built connectors and CDC frameworks do not handle: proprietary APIs with non-standard authentication, legacy systems that only expose data through screen scraping or mainframe interfaces, partner systems that deliver files in custom formats, or internal systems with unique data export mechanisms. Custom extraction means writing and maintaining your own extraction code. The strength is that it can handle anything. The limitation is that everything is your responsibility: error handling, retry logic, schema detection, incremental loading, and monitoring. This is the most expensive category to maintain over time, and the one you should revert to only as a last resort.

Choosing the connector

The source system profile from Chapter 2 provides the information needed to select the right connector category. The decision starts with the technical accessibility dimension and is refined based on the other profile scores.

If the source system supports log-based CDC, meaning it exposes a Write-Ahead Log or change stream, and the freshness requirement demands real-time or near-real-time data, the architectural choice is a CDC framework. This applies primarily to relational databases like PostgreSQL, MySQL, SQL Server, or Oracle that support transaction log access. The source must score high on technical accessibility for this path to be viable.

If the source system is a standard database, SaaS application, or cloud service, and the freshness requirement allows batch processing, a managed connector is almost always the right choice. The connector handles incremental loading, schema detection, and error handling out of the box. The data team configures rather than builds, which dramatically reduces setup time and ongoing maintenance. This covers the majority of enterprise source systems. Also, most cloud providers, such as Google, AWS, and Microsoft, have their own tools for that.

Source profile characteristics	Recommended connector category	Typical sources
Supports log-based CDC, real-time freshness needed	CDC framework (Debezium, Kafka Connect)	PostgreSQL, MySQL, SQL Server, Oracle, MongoDB
Standard system, API or database access available, batch freshness sufficient	Managed connector (Airbyte, dlt, Fivetran)	Salesforce, HubSpot, Google Analytics, Stripe, standard databases, SaaS APIs
Standard system, API available, real-time freshness needed but no log-based CDC	Managed connector with frequent scheduling or webhook-based triggers	SaaS APIs with webhook support, event-based cloud services
Non-standard interface, proprietary format, legacy system	Custom extraction	Mainframes, proprietary ERPs, partner file feeds, screen-scraping scenarios
File-based export only (CSV, XML, JSON to SFTP or cloud storage)	Managed connector or lightweight custom script if first doesn't work	Legacy batch exports, regulatory data feeds, external data providers

If the source system has low technical accessibility, meaning it only supports file exports, proprietary interfaces, or non-standard APIs, custom extraction becomes necessary. This is the path for legacy systems, mainframes, or partner data feeds that no pre-built connector supports. Before committing to custom extraction, it is worth checking whether the source team can improve the interface, which is exactly the conversation the source profile was designed to enable.

Things to look for in connectors

Regardless of which category applies, five capabilities separate reliable connector tooling from fragile solutions.

The first is schema detection and propagation. The connector should detect the source schema automatically and propagate changes when the schema evolves. This includes adding new columns, handling type changes gracefully, and alerting when columns are removed. Without this, every source schema change requires manual pipeline adjustment, which does not scale.

The second is incremental support. The connector should support delta loads natively, meaning it tracks what has already been synced and only extracts new or changed records. As discussed in the first volume, full loads should be a fallback, not the default. Incremental support reduces load on the source system, lowers network and compute costs, and shortens pipeline execution time.

The third is error handling and retry logic. Network failures, authentication timeouts, and source system downtime are not exceptions. The connector must handle transient failures through automatic retries with backoff, and it must report persistent failures clearly so the orchestration layer can respond. A connector that fails silently or requires manual restart after every hiccup is not fit for production.

The fourth is parallelism. For high-volume sources, the connector should be able to extract data from multiple tables or partitions concurrently. Sequential extraction becomes a bottleneck quickly when the source contains hundreds of tables or delivers large volumes per run.

The fifth is monitoring integration. The connector should emit metrics that feed into the monitoring and observability architecture we will describe later in this chapter. Extraction duration, row counts, error rates, and data volume should be available as signals without requiring custom instrumentation.

Build vs. Buy

The decision between pre-built and custom connectors deserves careful consideration, because the initial build cost of a custom connector is rarely the real expense. The real cost is maintenance.

Pre-built connectors, whether open-source or commercial, cover the most common source systems. Their communities or vendors handle updates when source APIs change, when security patches are needed, or when new features become available. This maintenance happens outside your team's capacity. For standard sources, using a pre-built connector is almost always the right choice, even if it does not cover every edge case. For edge cases, it is usually cheaper to build a plugin for a common connector than to build the whole thing from scratch.

Custom connectors become necessary when no pre-built option exists. This is appropriate for proprietary systems, unusual data formats, or legacy interfaces for which nobody else has built a connector. But the team must go in with open eyes. A custom connector is a piece of software that needs versioning, testing, error handling, monitoring, and ongoing maintenance as the source system evolves. In my experience, the initial build takes weeks to months, but the maintenance over the following years consumes significantly more engineering time than anyone estimated at the start. Avoid this and use custom connectors only in very limited cases. Custom connectors also tend to adopt a "fire and forget" mentality: they are budgeted once for development and then expected to run forever at no cost. But a custom connector is like any other piece of software you own; nobody would expect it to run for years without patches, upgrades, and maintenance.

The practical recommendation is to default to pre-built connectors for every source where one exists, invest in custom connectors only where there is genuinely no alternative, and treat every custom connector as technical debt to be replaced by a pre-built option as soon as one becomes available.

Orchestration architecture

In Volume 1, we introduced DAGs as the mechanism for managing dependencies between retrieval steps. We showed how tasks relate to each other and why the workflow must not contain cycles. Now we need to turn it into an architectural decision: what must the orchestration layer do, how should DAGs be structured for Data Products, and which architectural philosophy fits best?

What do we expect from orchestration?

Any orchestration architecture for Data Products must fulfill five requirements. They are the minimum that makes the retrieval pipeline from the previous section operationally viable. If you want to dive deep into this topic, I also recommend reading about ETL and ELT, as they serve as a vital baseline for what we discuss here.

The first is dependency management. Steps in the retrieval pipeline must execute in the correct order. Extraction must be completed before staging is processed. Validation must be completed before classification runs. This is the core DAG principle from Volume 1, but at the architectural level, it extends beyond a single pipeline. Some Data Products depend on data from other Data Products, and the orchestrator must be able to express and enforce these cross-product dependencies.

The second is idempotency. Any pipeline run must be safely re-executable without duplicating data in the source-aligned Data Product. When a run fails halfway through and needs to be restarted, the orchestrator must ensure that the records already written are not written again. Without idempotency, this becomes very challenging for engineers to roll back and determine what needs to be redone.

The third is retry and backoff. Transient failures are normal in distributed systems. A source system might be temporarily unavailable or a network call might time out. The orchestrator must handle these automatically through configurable retry strategies with increasing wait times between attempts. If a failure persists beyond the retry limit, it must be escalated as a hard failure, not retried indefinitely.

The fourth is failure isolation. A failed step in one Data Product's pipeline must not cascade into unrelated pipelines or steps. If the CRM extraction fails, it should not prevent the ERP extraction from running. Isolation ensures that a single source problem does not bring down the entire retrieval infrastructure.

The fifth is observability. Every pipeline run must emit metadata that feeds into the monitoring and audit logging architecture we defined in Chapter 2. The minimum includes run timestamps, step durations, success or failure status, row counts, and error messages. Without this, the orchestrator is a black box, and the governance controls from Chapter 2 have no data to work with.

How to structure DAGs for Data Products

The recommended approach is one DAG per Data Product. This creates clean isolation: each DAG is owned by a single team, serves a single product, and can be deployed, modified, and debugged independently. When a DAG fails, it is immediately clear which Data Product is affected and who is responsible.

The alternative, shared DAGs that orchestrate multiple Data Products in a single workflow, is tempting because it reduces the number of DAGs to manage. But it creates coupling. A failure in one product's extraction can block another product's entire pipeline. The maintenance overhead of shared DAGs grows faster than the overhead of managing separate ones. However, it is necessary to have an overview of which DAGs are in place to avoid replicating them and causing data inconsistencies. This approach also fits well with the principle of ownership: a team that owns a data product is responsible for its DAGs.

Cross-product dependencies do exist. A consumer-aligned Data Product might need data from multiple source-aligned products, and its processing should only start after all upstream extractions have completed. The architectural answer is not to merge everything into one DAG. Instead, cross-product dependencies should be managed through sensors or event triggers. A sensor waits for a signal that an upstream product's pipeline has completed successfully, then starts the dependent pipeline. This preserves isolation while respecting dependencies.

The DAG structure should be derivable from the ODPS YAML. The input ports in the YAML define which sources need extraction. The schedule defines when the DAG triggers. The quality rules define the validation step. This connection between the product definition and the orchestration is what makes the pipeline template from the previous section work in practice. However, the ODPS has no details about the DAG itself – don't try to pull it into the YAML file; a pipeline has its own definition. The ODPS only serves as a rough template.

Task-based versus asset-based orchestration

There are two architectural philosophies for orchestration, and they shape how the retrieval pipeline is expressed and managed.

The task-based approach, with Apache Airflow as its most prominent representative, thinks in terms of steps to execute. A DAG is a sequence of tasks: extract this table, validate that schema, and load these records. The orchestrator knows the order and the dependencies, but it does not inherently understand what data each task produces. Airflow is mature, has a vast ecosystem of pre-built operators and integrations, and is well understood by most data engineering teams. Its limitation for Data Products is that the concept of a data asset is implicit rather than explicit. The orchestrator manages tasks, and the team must maintain a mental map of the tasks and the Data Products they serve.

The asset-based approach, with Dagster as the leading example, thinks in terms of data assets to produce. A DAG is a directed acyclic graph in which each node represents a data output, not a task. The orchestrator understands that a source-aligned Data Product depends on extracted data from a specific source, and it manages the pipeline in terms of these assets rather than abstract tasks. This aligns more naturally with Data Product thinking, because the orchestrator speaks the same language as the ODPS definition: inputs, outputs, and dependencies between data assets.

Neither approach is categorically better. Airflow's maturity, community, and ecosystem make it a safe and capable choice.

Dagster's asset-oriented model is a more natural fit for Data Products but comes with a smaller ecosystem and less organizational familiarity. In many organizations, the choice is already made by existing investments. Migrating from one orchestrator to another is expensive and rarely justified unless the current tool fundamentally cannot meet the five requirements we defined above.

What matters more than the specific tool is that the orchestration architecture meets those requirements and that the DAG structure reflects the Data Product definition rather than evolving into an unmanageable tangle of ad-hoc dependencies. The tool is then just up to your organization's preferences.

Storage architecture

The retrieval pipeline ends with data landing in a source-aligned Data Product. This is the first tangible output of the entire retrieval process, and its storage architecture determines how well the governance controls from Chapter 2 and the pipeline design from this chapter actually work in practice. Get the storage architecture wrong, and reprocessing becomes painful, auditing becomes impossible, and downstream products inherit problems they should never have seen.

Storage zones for source-aligned products

The retrieval layer operates across three distinct storage zones, each with a different purpose and lifecycle.

The staging area is a transient buffer. Raw data lands here exactly as it was extracted, before any validation or classification. Staging exists solely to provide the pipeline with a place to hold data while it runs quality gates and applies classification labels. Once a pipeline run completes successfully, the staging data is automatically cleaned up. It is not a Data Product and thus not accessible by its consumers. It is an internal implementation detail of the pipeline that only exists while the pipeline is active.

The source-aligned Data Product is where validated, classified data lives permanently. This is the actual Data Product at the retrieval layer. It stores data close to how the source delivered it, with minimal transformation: type casting, encoding normalization, and standardized column naming where needed, but no business logic. The source-aligned product is the foundation that aggregated and consumer-aligned products build on later in the integration phase. However, the Data Product framing is more precise because it carries ownership, governance, and lifecycle management already, and thus brings value to its downstream consumers.

The quarantine zone is the parallel path for rejected data. When quality gates reject a batch or individual records, the rejected data lands here, along with the rejection reason, the rule that triggered the failure, and the pipeline run identifier. Quarantine is architecturally identical to the source-aligned product in storage format, just in a separate location with additional rejection metadata. It is a temporary holding area with its own retention policy, not a permanent archive.

Choosing the right format

The physical storage format for source-aligned Data Products is an architectural decision with long-term consequences. Three formats dominate the modern data landscape, and each comes with different trade-offs.

Parquet is the baseline. It is columnar, widely supported across virtually every data tool, offers strong compression, and handles large datasets efficiently. Its limitation is that it provides no built-in support for ACID transactions, time travel, or schema enforcement. If you need to reprocess data or query a previous version, you must manage that yourself through partitioning conventions and manual versioning.

Delta Lake builds on Parquet and adds what Parquet lacks: ACID transactions, time travel through versioned snapshots, schema enforcement, and schema evolution support. For source-aligned products, Delta Lake is a strong fit because it natively supports the immutability and reprocessing requirements we will discuss below. Time travel means you can always query the state of the product as it was at any point in the past, which directly supports auditing and debugging. Delta Lake is closely associated with the Databricks ecosystem but can be used independently.

Apache Iceberg offers similar capabilities to Delta Lake: ACID transactions, time travel, and schema evolution, but with a vendor-neutral design and growing adoption across multiple platforms. Iceberg's partition evolution feature is particularly useful: you can change the partitioning strategy of existing data without rewriting it, which matters when volume patterns shift over time. Iceberg has strong momentum in the broader open-source ecosystem beyond any single vendor. I saw this format especially when the company has a multi-vendor strategy.

The choice depends primarily on the existing platform. If the organization uses Databricks, Delta Lake is the natural fit. If the organization values vendor neutrality or uses a multi-platform setup, Iceberg is the stronger choice. If the environment is simple and does not require transactions or time travel, Parquet alone can work, but the team must accept the operational overhead of manually managing versioning and schema enforcement.

Capability	Delta Lake	Apache Iceberg
Columnar storage	Yes (Parquet-based)	Yes (Parquet-based)
ACID transactions	Yes	Yes
Time travel	Yes	Yes
Schema enforcement	Yes	Yes
Schema evolution	Yes	Yes
Partition evolution	No (requires rewrite)	Yes
Vendor neutrality	Medium (Databricks-linked)	High
Ecosystem breadth	Wide	Growing rapidly

Partitioning strategies

Partitioning determines how data is physically organized in storage. The right strategy improves query performance and keeps file sizes manageable. The wrong strategy creates thousands of tiny files that degrade performance or a few massive files that are expensive to process. Whatever system you use has different capabilities for this. I won't give any recommendations here, as this would differ too much by system.

Over-partitioning is a common mistake. A source that delivers 10,000 records per day does not need partitioning by date, source, or region. That creates dozens of partitions with a few hundred records each, resulting in many small files that storage engines handle poorly. The important thing is to find the sweet spot in the file size. Small files receive too many concurrent requests, which are difficult to handle, and large files reduce the ability to process them in parallel.

Schema-on-write for source-aligned products

There are two schools of thought on when to enforce schema. Schema-on-read accepts everything into storage and interprets the structure at query time. Schema-on-write enforces the expected schema at ingestion time and rejects data that does not conform.

For source-aligned Data Products, the recommendation is schema-on-write. The reasoning is straightforward: we already have quality gates that validate the schema as part of the pipeline. If data passes the gate, it conforms to the expected structure. Enforcing the schema at write time is simply the storage-level expression of what the gate already validated. This prevents malformed data from ever entering the product, even if the gate logic has a gap.

Schema-on-read has its place in exploratory environments where the structure is genuinely unknown. But source-aligned products are not exploratory. They receive data from profiled sources with known schemas. Accepting anything and sorting it out later defeats the purpose of the governance architecture we built in Chapter 2.

Why source-aligned products must be immutable

Once data is written to a source-aligned Data Product, it is never overwritten. New data is appended. Corrections are expressed as new records, not as modifications to existing ones. This principle of immutability is non-negotiable for three reasons.

The first is reprocessing. If downstream transformation logic changes, we need the ability to rerun the integration phase from the source-aligned product without reverting to the source system. Immutability guarantees that the original ingested data is always available as the starting point for reprocessing. The second is auditing. The audit trail from Chapter 2 proves what was ingested and when. If the underlying data can be overwritten, the audit trail becomes meaningless because the data it references no longer exists in its original form. Immutability ensures that the audit record and the data it describes remain consistent. The third is debugging. When a downstream consumer reports incorrect data, the investigation starts at the source-aligned product. If the product is immutable, we can always see exactly what was ingested and compare it against what the consumer received. If the product allows overwrites, a later ingestion run may have destroyed the original evidence.

Immutability does increase storage costs over time, because data accumulates rather than being replaced. This is where the retention policies from Chapter 2 come in. Data that has passed its retention period is archived or deleted according to the policy. Immutability and retention are complementary: we keep everything for as long as the policy requires, and we never modify what we keep.

Where quality gates and schema validation live in the architecture

In Chapter 2, we defined what quality gates do: they accept, flag, or reject data based on rules for completeness, validity, uniqueness, freshness, and volume. We defined the differences between hard and soft gates, between fail-all and fail-row strategies, and designed the quarantine zone for rejected data. What we did not define is where these components sit in the architecture and how they connect to the pipeline and storage layers we just described.

Architectural placement

Quality gates are a mandatory step in the retrieval pipeline, sitting between the staging area and the source-aligned Data Product. No data moves from staging into the product without passing through the gate. Treat this as your main architectural constraint. If the gate can be bypassed, it will be bypassed, and the governance controls from Chapter 2 become meaningless. Schema validation runs first, before any data quality rules execute. It compares the incoming schema against the expected schema stored in the Data Contract. One note here: we haven't discussed the Data Contract yet, as it's covered in Volume 3 of the series. The contract registry is a dedicated architectural component that holds the current expected schema for each input port, derived from the ODPS definition. When the pipeline-based update process from Chapter 1 introduces a planned schema change, the registry is updated as part of that process. Unplanned schema changes, where the incoming schema differs from the registry without a corresponding update, are treated as schema drift and trigger an immediate hard gate failure. The entire batch is rejected because a structural mismatch affects every record.

Only after schema validation passes do the data quality rules execute. These rules are configured per input port and calibrated against the source system profile, as described in Chapter 2. The gate evaluates each rule and produces the routing decision: records or batches that pass go to the source-aligned Data Product, those that fail go to the quarantine zone.

Routing architecture

The gate strategy determines the routing between source-aligned product and quarantine. For fail-all rules, the decision is binary: the entire batch either goes to the product or to quarantine. For fail-row rules, the pipeline splits the batch. Conforming rows are written to the source-aligned product; non-conforming rows are written to quarantine with the rejection reason and rule identifier attached as metadata. Both paths produce identical metadata and audit records. A pipeline run that routes some records to quarantine appears in the monitoring dashboard is logged in the audit trail and is visible in the catalog as an operational quality metric on the Data Product.

The quarantine zone is architecturally identical to the source-aligned product in storage format. It uses the same file format, the same partitioning by ingestion date, and the same immutability principle. The only differences are the location and the additional rejection metadata. This design ensures that reprocessing quarantined data through the same pipeline is straightforward: once the underlying issue is resolved, quarantined records can re-enter the validation step and, if they pass, flow into the source-aligned product as if they had passed originally.

The metadata and lineage architecture

In Chapter 2, we designed the metadata sidecar that every pipeline run emits and the lineage records that track data from source to source-aligned product. We described what gets captured and why it matters. This section defines where that information lives architecturally and what the central component, the data catalog, must be capable of.

The catalog as the central hub

The data catalog is the architectural component that connects everything we have built across Chapters 1, 2, and 3. It is where the ODPS definition becomes discoverable for consumers. It is where the metadata sidecar from every pipeline run lands and where lineage is rendered visually. It is where classification labels, quality gate statistics, and freshness information are visible and where the catalog-based update process from Chapter 1 originates. For this to work, the catalog must be API-first. The metadata sidecar is pushed programmatically after every pipeline run, rather than entered manually in a UI. Schema snapshots, quality gate results, classification labels, lineage references, and run timestamps all arrive via API. If the catalog does not support automated ingestion through an API, the entire automation chain from Chapter 2 breaks down, and we are back to manual documentation that goes stale within weeks. Luckily, all modern Data Catalogs do expose APIs.

Beyond API support, the catalog must render lineage visually, at a minimum at the table level and ideally at the column level for regulated data. It must support search and discovery so consumers can find Data Products by name, domain, tag, or classification level. It must integrate with the ODPS standard, either by ingesting ODPS YAML directly or by mapping its fields to the catalog's internal model. And it must enforce the role-based permissions we defined in Chapter 1 for catalog-based updates.

How the pipeline connects to the catalog

The metadata sidecar is the bridge between the pipeline and the catalog. After each pipeline run, the orchestration layer pushes the sidecar record to the catalog via API. This single push delivers schema snapshots that enable drift detection over time, quality gate results that appear as operational quality metrics on the Data Product, classification labels that drive access controls, and run metadata that powers freshness monitoring.

Lineage at the retrieval layer is captured from two sources: Table-level lineage comes from the DAG definition, and pipeline run context (which source system, which pipeline, which target location). This is available from any orchestrator. Column-level lineage is determined by the connector's schema mapping, which specifies which source column maps to which target column. Not all connectors expose this, which is why I recommended table-level lineage as the default and column-level as a selective addition for regulated data.

Reference architectures

Two open-source projects represent the current state of catalog and lineage architecture. DataHub offers push-based metadata ingestion, strong lineage visualization, and broad integration with orchestrators and data platforms. OpenMetadata provides native data quality integration, an ODPS-friendly structure, and a growing connector ecosystem. Both implement the same architectural pattern: the catalog as a central metadata store with API-based ingestion, lineage rendering, and search. The choice between them, or any other catalog tool, depends on integration fit with the existing orchestrator and storage layer, not on feature lists. A catalog that integrates cleanly with your orchestrator and file format will deliver value immediately.

There are also a large number of very mature commercial Data Catalogs. This book isn't about Data Catalogs. Rather, we see them as an integral part of Data Products. Whatever tool you select is the right one for your use case!

Monitoring and observability

In Chapter 2, we designed the audit trail as an immutable compliance record of what happened to data. Monitoring serves a different purpose. It answers whether the retrieval infrastructure is healthy right now and whether action is needed. Both feed from the same pipeline events, but they serve different audiences, have different retention requirements, and must be stored separately.

What to monitor

Monitoring for retrieval pipelines comprises three layers that provide a clear view of the state of our Data Product. Pipeline health tracks whether pipelines run successfully, how long they take, and how often they retry. A pipeline that succeeded but took three times as long as usual is a warning signal, even though nothing technically failed. Trending duration upward over weeks often indicates a growing volume problem or a degrading source system before it causes an outright failure. It is necessary to track these changes to act on them. If the source system is the issue, you would even be able to tell the producers that "something is going on".

Data health tracks the signals that quality gates and metadata capture already produce: volume anomalies, freshness, and gate pass rates. A sudden drop in row count might mean the source system had an issue; a spike in soft gate flags might indicate gradual quality degradation at the source. A freshness violation occurs when the source-aligned Data Product serves stale data to downstream consumers. These signals exist because we built them into the pipeline architecture; monitoring makes them visible and actionable.

Infrastructure health tracks storage growth, compute utilization, and connector throughput. A steadily growing quarantine zone signals unresolved quality problems and storage costs that increase faster than the number of Data Products suggests, indicating a retention policy that is not executing or a partitioning strategy that creates excessively small files.

Designing the alerting topology

Not every monitoring signal deserves an alert. The fastest way to make a team ignore all alerts is to flood them with noise. The alerting topology must distinguish three levels. Critical alerts require immediate action. A pipeline failure that blocks data from reaching the source-aligned product, a hard gate rejection that sends an entire batch to quarantine, or a source system that becomes unavailable during extraction are all critical. These go to the data engineering team immediately, because the Data Product is not receiving fresh data until someone intervenes.

Warning alerts require review during business hours. Elevated retry counts, soft gate flags, volume deviations outside the normal range, or duration increases that suggest emerging problems are warnings. These go to a monitoring channel where the team reviews them as part of their daily routine, not as interruptions. Informational signals are visible on dashboards but do not trigger notifications. Successful pipeline runs, normal volume variation, and routine performance metrics belong here. They provide context when investigating an issue but do not require attention on their own.

Who receives which alert matters as much as the alert itself. Pipeline and infrastructure issues go to the data engineering team, while quality and freshness issues go to the Data Product Owner, because they affect the product's consumers and may require coordination with the source system team. Sending every alert to everyone ensures no one reads any of them.

Key learnings

- **Five stages, one template**: Every retrieval pipeline follows the same architecture: extraction, staging, validation, classification, and loading. All of this with a parallel quarantine path for rejected data. Design the template once and parameterize it per Data Product. New products configure an instance; they do not build from scratch.

- **Choose connectors based on the source profile, not on hype**: CDC frameworks for real-time needs with log-based sources, managed connectors for standard systems and batch freshness, custom extraction only as a last resort. Every custom connector is technical debt that should be replaced as soon as a pre-built option becomes available.

- **One DAG per Data Product:** Isolation prevents cascading failures; cross-product dependencies are managed through event triggers, not by merging everything into one massive workflow. The DAG structure should reflect the ODPS definition.

- **Source-aligned products must be immutable**: Append-only, never overwrite. Immutability enables reprocessing when transformation logic changes, keeps the audit trail meaningful, and preserves the evidence needed for debugging. Retention policies manage storage costs over time.

- **Monitoring is not auditing**: The audit trail proves what happened for compliance. Monitoring tells you whether something needs attention right now. Both feed from the same pipeline events but serve different audiences and different retention requirements. And the fastest way to make a team ignore all alerts is to send every alert to everyone.

FOUR

The P in Retrieval

In Volume 1, we dedicated significant attention to the people dimension. We defined the roles needed for Data Product delivery: the Data Product Owner, the Squad Lead, the Tech Lead, and the various engineering roles. We designed organizational structures using the Hub-and-Spoke model and the Spotify-inspired squad setup. We covered change management, resistance, and the importance of stakeholder buy-in. And we established a principle that runs through everything: you can implement the best tools, platforms, and governance structures, but if people resist using them, the initiative will fail.

In Chapters 2 and 3, we built the governance framework and the data retrieval architecture. But both chapters left a critical question unanswered: "Who actually operates all of this?" The source system profile from Chapter 2 has an ownership and contact dimension, but what does the conversation with that source team actually look like? The quality gates need calibration, but who decides the thresholds and who recalibrates when things change? The architecture chapter designed a reusable pipeline template, but who builds it, who parameterizes it for each new Data Product, and who responds when monitoring raises an alert?

This chapter answers these questions. It is not about defining new roles or redesigning the organization. Volume 1 did that—or, at least, defined the roles. It is about mapping the people who already exist to the specific activities that enable retrieval. The governance rules from Chapter 2 need humans to enforce them. The architecture from Chapter 3 needs humans to operate it. This chapter is the operating model that connects people to both.

Figure 7 shows who is involved in the retrieval phase and how they interact. The Data Product team sits at the center, but it cannot work in isolation. It depends on source system IT teams for access and schema stability, on business unit owners for domain knowledge and descriptive metadata, on finance and controlling for the financial gate we introduced in Chapter 1, and on consumers who ultimately determine whether the Data Product delivers value. Each of these relationships carries specific responsibilities, and we will work through them in the sections that follow.

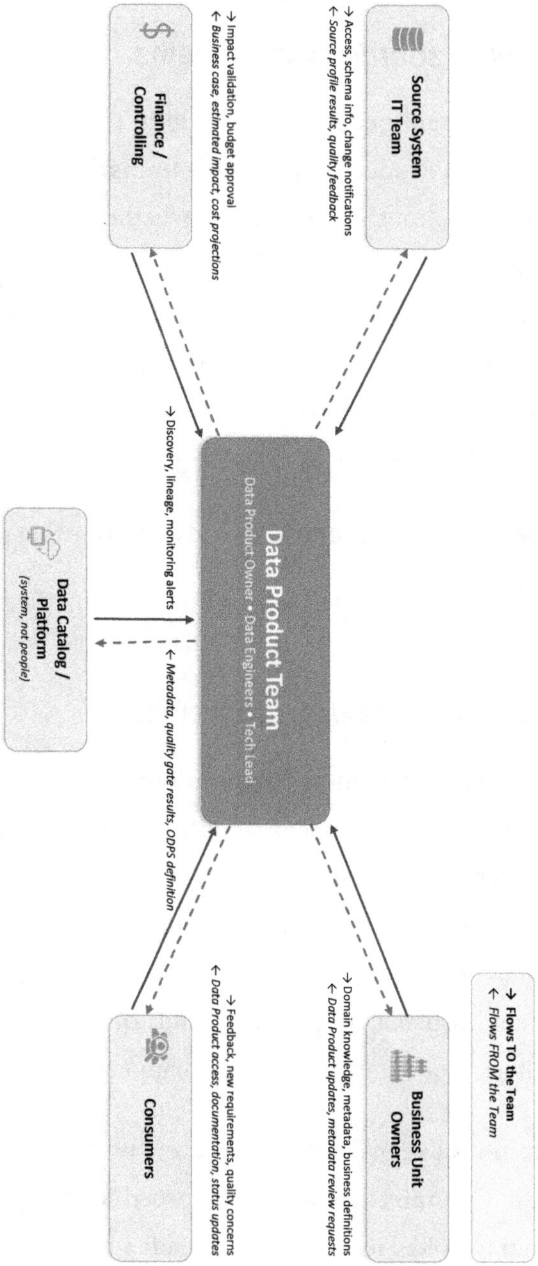

Figure 7: Retrieval phase involvement.

Working with source system teams

The most important people relationship in the retrieval phase is between the Data Product team and the teams that own the source systems. This relationship determines whether the source system profile from Chapter 2 gets filled with useful information or with guesswork. It determines whether schema changes are communicated before they break your pipeline or after. And it determines whether data quality issues get fixed at the source or papered over downstream.

In my experience, this relationship is also the one that goes wrong most often.

"We just dump the data somewhere"

Source system teams, in most organizations, care about one thing: the application. They care about uptime. They care about user experience. They care about the software design. What they rarely care about is the data model underneath. The data model is a by-product. It emerged organically over years of feature development, schema migrations, and quick fixes. Nobody designed it as a coherent whole. It just happened.

The result looks like 3NF on the surface, but it is a Frankenstein underneath. Columns that were repurposed for things they were never meant to hold. Field names that made sense to whoever built them five years ago but mean nothing to anyone else.

Relationships that exist in application code but not in the schema. Tables that started as temporary workarounds and became permanent fixtures. When you ask the source team about their data model, the answer is often a shrug: "We just dump the data somewhere. The application handles the rest."

This attitude is not malicious. It is rational from the source team's perspective. Their job is to build and run the application, not to serve downstream data consumers. In Volume 1, we established that data quality starts at the source, with the POS system example and the call center story.

In reality, source system teams rarely see data quality as their responsibility.
They see it as someone else's problem.
And that someone is you.

This is why the source system profiling exercise from Chapter 2 is not just a technical assessment. It is the beginning of a relationship. And like any relationship, it requires communication, trust, and a clear understanding of what each side needs from the other.

How to approach the profiling conversation

The profiling conversation works best when it is framed as collaboration, not as an audit. Source system teams become defensive when they feel inspected. They become cooperative when they feel included. Those are people skills everyone needs in data.

The practical approach is to start with what you need, not with what they are doing wrong. Instead of "your data quality is poor and we need to understand why," try "we are building a Data Product that depends on your system, and we need your help to understand how the data behaves." The first framing creates resistance, whereas the second creates partnership.

During the profiling conversation, the Data Product team should walk through the seven dimensions from Chapter 2 together with the source team. The source team knows things that no amount of data profiling can reveal: why certain fields have high null rates (because the field was added later and never backfilled), why the schema changes unpredictably (because the team deploys continuously without a formal release cycle), or why volume spikes at month's end (because a batch job reconciles the entire ledger).

This knowledge is invaluable. It turns the source system profile, a set of measured numbers, into a document that explains why the numbers look the way they do. And it builds the foundation for an ongoing working relationship that will matter every time the source system changes.

Establishing ongoing communication

The profiling conversation is a starting point, not a one-time event. The most critical ongoing need is communication about changes. In Chapter 2, we identified schema stability as a key profiling dimension. In Chapter 3, we designed schema validation as the first quality gate. But both of these are defensive measures. They detect problems after they happen. The better approach is to prevent problems by knowing about changes before they arrive.

This requires an agreement with the source team. The agreement does not need to be a formal contract; it is a practical understanding: when you plan a schema change, you tell us in advance. When you schedule a major migration, you give us a heads-up. When you know your system will be down for maintenance, let us know so we can adjust our pipeline schedule.

In Volume 1, we discussed how the Hub-and-Spoke model assigns platform ownership to the Hub and data ownership to the Spokes. Source system teams typically sit in the Spokes or in IT teams that serve specific business units. The Data Product team, often anchored in the Hub, needs a communication channel to these teams. This can be as simple as a shared Slack channel, a regular sync meeting, or a notification process tied to the source team's deployment pipeline.

What matters is not the format but the commitment. If the source team sees the Data Product team as an important downstream consumer, they will communicate with the Data Product team. If they see data extraction as an afterthought, they will not. Building that awareness is the Data Product team's responsibility, and it starts during the profiling conversation.

A practical collaboration agreement

To formalize this working relationship without creating bureaucracy, I recommend a lightweight collaboration agreement between the Data Product team and each source system team. This is not a data contract in the technical sense; it is a people agreement that captures the essentials.

The agreement should cover five points. First, a contact list: who on the source team is the technical contact for schema questions, and who is the escalation point when things go wrong. Second, a change notification commitment: the source team agrees to notify the Data Product team before planned schema changes or major system updates, with a minimum lead time. Third, a maintenance window schedule: when the source system is regularly unavailable, the pipeline schedule can account for it. Fourth, a data quality baseline acknowledgment: both teams agree on the current quality baseline from the source profile, ensuring a shared understanding of what "normal" looks like. Fifth, an escalation path: "When an issue arises that cannot be resolved between the two teams, who should be involved next?"

This agreement normally goes somewhere close to the Data Product, ideally in the Data Catalog for the Data Product. It could also be in the Git repository, as developers look this up there.

Responsibilities in the data retrieval phase

In Volume 1, we defined the roles for Data Product delivery: the Data Product Owner, the Tech Lead, data engineers, and domain experts. Chapters 2 and 3 introduced many retrieval activities but left it open who is responsible for each. This section closes that gap with a RACI matrix that maps existing roles to retrieval-specific responsibilities.

RACI assigns four levels: Responsible (does the work), Accountable (owns the work), Consulted (provides input), and Informed (needs to know). The following table provides a guideline that can be adapted to your organization.

Three patterns matter here. The Data Product Owner is accountable for governance decisions: profiling, classification, retention, audit, reflecting Volume 1's principle that ownership of the product includes ownership of its quality. But the hands-on work falls to the Data Engineer, who is responsible for most technical activities. Also note that the domain expert (business users) is always involved here, as I see data quality as a joint effort.

Retrieval activity	Data Product Owner	Data Engineer	Tech Lead	Domain Expert	Source System Team
Source system profiling (Ch. 2)	A	R	C	C	C
Collaboration agreement (Ch. 4)	A	R	C	I	R
Connector selection (Ch. 3)	I	R	A	-	C
Pipeline configuration (Ch. 3)	I	R	A	-	I
Quality gate rules and calibration (Ch. 2)	C	R	A	R	-
Classification setup (Ch. 2)	A	R	C	C	C
Descriptive metadata authoring (Ch. 2)	A	I	-	R	C
Technical metadata and lineage (Ch. 2)	I	R	A	-	-
Monitoring and alerting (Ch. 3)	C	R	A	-	-
Alert response: pipeline issues (Ch. 3)	A	R	C	-	C
Alert response: quality issues (Ch. 3)	R	C	A	C	I
Retention and audit (Ch. 2)	A	R	C	I	

The Tech Lead is accountable for architectural decisions across connectors, pipeline configuration, gate design, and monitoring.

The Domain Expert is critical for two activities nobody else can do: authoring descriptive metadata and providing business context during profiling and gate calibration. Without a Domain Expert assigned, these activities will not happen, and the Data Product will lack the business meaning that makes it usable. We will explore this challenge in detail later in this chapter.

The most common failure mode this table prevents is overloading the Data Engineer. In many organizations, data engineers end up doing everything: profiling, writing metadata, calibrating thresholds, and responding to alerts. The RACI makes clear that while data engineers execute most technical work, accountability and domain knowledge must come from others. A data engineer who is also expected to write business definitions for fields they do not understand will produce metadata that is incorrect or fluffy.

Training source system users for data quality

Data quality starts at the source, and the source is people. We told the story of call center agents who were measured on handling time and call volume, which made logging call reasons a burden rather than a priority. We described POS system operators who are under pressure during customer interactions and see structured data entry as a tedious afterthought. In both cases, the fix was not more downstream validation. It was investing in the people who create the data: better training, simpler interfaces, and aligned incentives.

The source system profile from Chapter 2 provides a quality baseline with concrete numbers: null rates, duplicate rates, and format inconsistencies. These numbers are the business case for training. When the profile shows that 15% of customer records have missing email addresses, we can calculate the downstream costs: failed campaign targeting, incomplete analytics, and manual cleanup effort. This turns "we should improve data entry" from a vague aspiration into a quantifiable investment.

Training itself must be practical and low-friction. The people entering data in source systems are not data professionals. They are sales agents, customer service representatives, warehouse operators, or shop employees. They will not attend a two-hour workshop on data quality theory. What works is short, focused interventions tied to their daily workflow. Show them what happens when they skip a field: not in abstract data quality terms, but in terms they care about. "When you leave the email field empty, marketing cannot reach this customer, and your team's campaign performance drops." Connect data entry to outcomes that matter to them. Here, it is helpful to work closely with managers in their departments to understand what matters to employees. It is very important to connect with their daily work struggles; otherwise, they won't relate to it. This, in turn, means your data problems won't be solved.

Equally important is fixing the systems, not just the people. In Volume 1, we described how reducing the number of selectable options in the call center software led to significant quality improvements within months. The same principle applies broadly: if the interface makes it easy to enter data correctly and hard to enter it incorrectly, training reinforces good behavior rather than fighting bad design. This is a conversation between the Data Product team and the source system IT team from earlier in this chapter, because interface improvements require collaboration between both sides.

The results should be measurable. After training, re-run the quality profiling from Chapter 2 and compare. If the null rate on customer email dropped from 15% to 5%, the training worked. If it did not, either the training missed the mark or the system design still makes it too difficult to make a correct entry. Either way, the source profile gives you the evidence to iterate, and iterating on data quality at the source is the cheapest quality investment in the entire Data Product lifecycle.

In my experience, I have gained most of the benefits here. This is a part where few costly software investments are necessary, and thus it is low-hanging fruit.

Building descriptive metadata with business

No pipeline will turn a column named "fname" into a clear business definition. Someone who understands the business must write these descriptions. The question is "Who?"

Descriptive metadata is business knowledge. And here lies the complexity that many Data Product initiatives underestimate: a source system is owned by one or more business units, who define what the data means, but it is operated and built by IT teams, who control how the data is structured and stored. The business side knows that "fname" means "full customer name, first name followed by optional middle name followed by last name." The IT side knows it is a VARCHAR(255) that is nullable. The Data Product team needs both, from different people, through different conversations.

Remember when we discussed the Hub-and-Spoke setup in Volume 1? This is highly relevant here: business units own the meaning, the Hub owns the technical standards. For descriptive metadata during the retrieval phase, this means the Data Product Owner is accountable and the Domain Expert is responsible, as shown in our RACI table. The moment to capture this knowledge is during the Data Product definition phase from Chapter 1, not after the pipeline is already running. Once the product is in production, getting business people to retroactively document field meanings becomes exponentially harder.

To keep it practical: provide templates with examples, not empty forms. Show the Domain Expert a completed description for a similar field and ask them to do the same. Use the staleness alerts from Chapter 2 to flag fields that still lack descriptions after the product goes live. And accept that descriptive metadata will never be complete on day one. What matters is that it improves continuously, which is exactly what CIA (Continuous Improvement and Adaptation) was designed for.

Escalation and incident response

Chapter 3 designed the monitoring architecture and defined who gets which alerts: the data engineering team for pipeline and infrastructure issues, the Data Product Owner for quality and freshness issues. But an alert is not a resolution. Someone must triage, act, and communicate. This section defines that flow.

When a critical alert fires, the first responder is always the data engineer on the squad. Their job is triage: "Is this a pipeline problem, a source system problem, or a data quality problem?" Pipeline problems, such as failed connectors or orchestration errors, are resolved within the team. Source system problems, such as an unavailable system or an unannounced schema change, require immediate contact with the source system team through the collaboration agreement from earlier in this chapter. Data quality problems, such as a hard-gate rejection caused by a sudden spike in null values, require investigation to determine whether the issue lies at the source or in the quality rules themselves.

If the issue cannot be resolved within the defined timeframe, escalation follows the RACI outlined earlier. The data engineer escalates technical decisions to the Tech Lead, such as whether to temporarily relax a quality gate threshold. The Data Product Owner escalates to the business when the product's freshness or availability is compromised, because consumers need to know that the data they rely on is stale or incomplete. In Volume 1, we discussed how transparency builds trust. Hiding a retrieval failure from consumers until they notice it themselves is the fastest way to destroy that trust.

The Data Product Owner is accountable for communicating this to consumers. After resolution, a brief post-mortem captures what happened, why, and what changes prevent recurrence. This might be an update to the collaboration agreement, a recalibrated quality gate threshold, or a change request to the source system team. The post-mortem feeds into the CIA cycle from the framework: every incident is an opportunity to make the Data Product more robust.

Key learnings

- **The source team relationship makes or breaks retrieval**: Approach source system profiling as collaboration, not as an audit. Source teams become defensive when they feel inspected and cooperative when they feel included. Start with what you need, not with what they are doing wrong.

- **Formalize the working relationship without creating bureaucracy**: A lightweight collaboration agreement covers five essentials. Store it in the catalog or the Git repository, not in someone's inbox.
- **Map existing roles to retrieval activities using a RACI**: The most common failure mode is overloading the Data Engineer with everything, including tasks that require domain knowledge they do not have.
- **Training source system users is the cheapest quality investment**: Connect data entry to outcomes that matter to the people entering the data. Use the source system profile to quantify the cost of poor data entry and fix the systems alongside the people.
- **Descriptive metadata requires business people, not engineers**: No pipeline will turn unclear naming into a clear business definition. Capture this knowledge during the Data Product definition phase, not after the product is in production.
- **Every incident is an opportunity to improve**: The data engineer triages, the Tech Lead makes architectural calls,

and the Data Product Owner communicates to consumers.

FIVE

The Sample Project

It's a Tuesday morning in late spring. Anna, the CDO of MCC, is looking at a dashboard she does not trust. Three recalls in eighteen months. Every post-mortem reaches the same conclusion: the signals were there, weeks before the recall was announced. A batch of brake pads from a supplier showed a higher defect rate than usual. Dealer service tickets for the same model started clustering around the same complaint code. And the assembly line telemetry for the affected VINs showed torque readings drifting out of spec.

All this data was sitting in source systems. Only downside: the data was owned by three different teams, in three different formats. Nobody had put it together because nobody could. Each system had its own access rules, its own export quirks, its own definition of what a "batch" even meant. By the time someone manually stitched together a spreadsheet, the cars were already on the road, and the disaster was unfolding.

Anna does what CDOs do in this situation: she commissions a Data Product initiative. The brief, written on a single slide: *we need supplier quality, dealer service, and manufacturing telemetry in one place, trustworthy, and kept current so the next pattern gets caught before it becomes a recall. The cost of a single recall runs to about 150 million.* The initial timeline is aggressive and the budget is real. This is where Chapter 5 picks up. We are the team Anna just hired, and our target is to make this Data Product a success. Over the rest of this chapter, we will do for MCC exactly what Chapters 1 through 4 described in the abstract:

- We will profile the three source systems.
- We will define three Data Products using ODPS.
- We will build the retrieval pipelines, one per source, using the same template.
- We will classify, apply quality gates, capture metadata, track lineage, and set up monitoring.
- We will work through a collaboration agreement with the manufacturing team and map responsibilities with a RACI.

The data concerns cars, and the source systems are within a car company. The consequences of getting the retrieval phase wrong are measured in recalls, warranty costs, and customer trust. A note on what this chapter is *not*:

- We will not build an aggregated Data Product that joins the three sources.
- We will not train a model that predicts recalls.

- We will not expose dashboards to Anna's executive team.
- We will not list the code line by line – this would be simply too much for a book.

What we build in this chapter is the foundation that each one of those downstream products will rely on: three source-aligned Data Products, governed, observable, and production-ready. Get this right, and everything downstream becomes possible. Get this wrong, and no model, dashboard, or data space will save Anna and MCC.

The tools we will use are all open source. I made this decision deliberately so you can work on the samples from chapter to chapter. The infrastructure runs on a single laptop with Docker and the data is synthetic but realistic. Everything you see in this chapter, you can run yourself. The data is available at https://cloudvane.at/book. You need to register and use the code "DPV2ACC" to get access. You will find two files. Register your email and verify it. Once that is done, I will add you to the Git repository and you can pull the samples. Let's get to work.

What we build

Before we start configuring tools, let's look at Figure 8 to see what we are building. One diagram, referenced throughout the chapter.

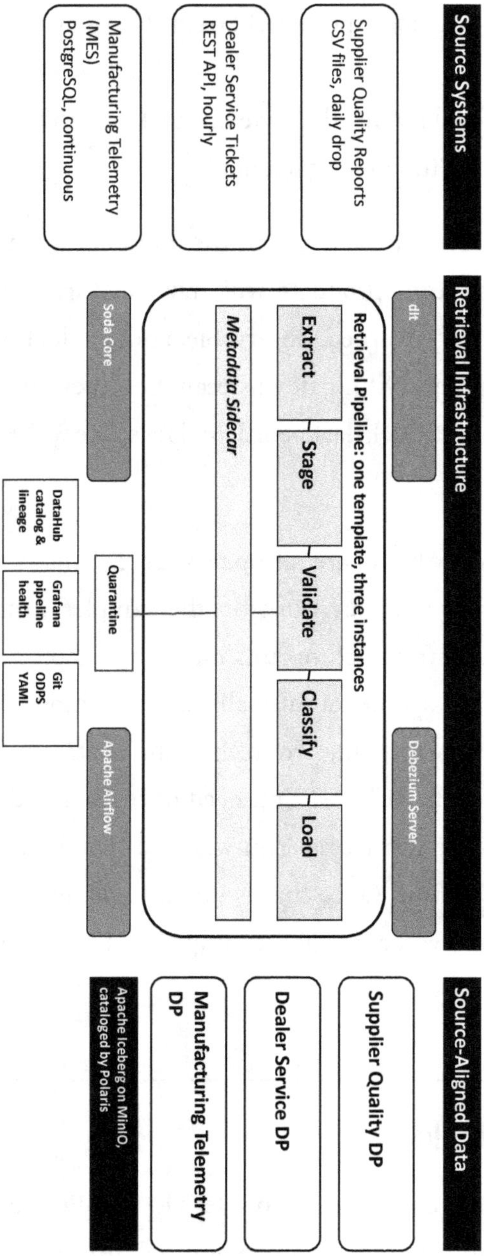

Figure 8: Case study architecture.

Three source systems on the left and three source-aligned Data Products on the right. Everything in between is the retrieval infrastructure from Chapter 3, instantiated with concrete open-source tools. The three source systems, where each one represents a different category of source from the initial description:

- **Supplier quality reports:** Files delivered daily by our parts suppliers. CSV format, dropped into an SFTP-like bucket. A partner-delivered source that we do not control.

- **Dealer Service Tickets:** Data from our dealer management system, exposed through a REST API. An internal system we control but access like any SaaS.

- **Manufacturing Telemetry (MES):** Events from the assembly line, written to a PostgreSQL database by our Manufacturing Execution System. High volume, needs to be fresh.

Each source requires a different extraction pattern from Volume 1. Supplier Quality gets a file-based batch. Dealer Service receives a timestamp-based delta via an API. Manufacturing Telemetry gets a log-based CDC. One sample project, three connector categories from Chapter 3. If you have built retrieval before, one of these three will feel familiar.

The three source-aligned Data Products. On the right side of the diagram, each source lands in its own source-aligned Data

Product. They are stored in Apache Iceberg tables, on MinIO object storage, with Polaris as the Iceberg catalog. Each Data Product has its own ODPS YAML, quality rules, retention policy, and lifecycle. They do not share storage with each other and they do not share pipelines with each other. The only thing they share is the template.

The retrieval infrastructure is in the middle. Five components do the work:

- **Apache Airflow** orchestrates the pipelines. One DAG per Data Product, as we learned in Chapter 3.

- **dlt** handles extraction for the file and API sources. A managed connector, Python-native, configured in code.

- **Debezium Server** handles CDC for the PostgreSQL source. Single binary, no Kafka cluster to operate.

- **Soda Core** runs the quality gates. YAML-defined rules, executed as an Airflow task.

- **DataHub** is the catalog. It receives the metadata sidecar after every pipeline run, renders lineage, and shows schema snapshots over time. DataHub runs in its own Docker container because it requires many services. Also, ensure you create a PAT (Personal Access Token), which is necessary for all other services to access DataHub.

Cross-cutting concerns. A small Grafana instance reads Airflow's metadata database and shows pipeline health. Classification is handled by shared Python code that every pipeline imports. Retention policies live in YAML alongside the ODPS files. The quarantine zone is a dedicated MinIO bucket that mirrors the source-aligned product structure, with extra rejection-reason columns.

It is important to mention that this setup doesn't represent my recommendation, nor should you read it as my preferred tools (especially no tool vendors, please!). Rather, it is a pragmatic solution to teach you how to develop Data Products. You could swap dlt with Airbyte or Fivetran, the results would be the same. Or exchange Soda with Great Expectations, you will also reach your goals. Also, consider this not a working, production-ready environment. This would need much more hardening, security, and reliability built into it. The goal of this setup is to show you the end-to-end process for a Data Product.

One rule that runs through everything. The ODPS YAML is the source of truth. The pipeline reads from it and the catalog entry is generated from it. If you want to change how a Data Product behaves, you change the YAML. Nothing in the pipelines should be hardcoded; it should live in the product definition. This is the principle from Chapter 1.

Now that we have the picture, let's look at the stack in more detail.

The open-source stack at a glance

Every tool in this chapter is open source. No trials, no license keys, no cloud accounts. Everything runs locally. This was my goal for the chapter: to make it easy to use.

The table below summarizes the stack, what each tool does, and which chapter of this book introduced the concept it implements.

Layer	Tool	What it does here	Concept from
Source database (MES)	PostgreSQL 16	Hosts the manufacturing telemetry table, exposes its Write-Ahead Log for CDC.	Ch. 3, extraction
Source API (Dealer)	FastAPI	Serves synthetic dealer tickets over REST with pagination and updated_since filter.	Ch. 3, extraction
Source files (Supplier)	MinIO bucket supplier-drop	Simulates a partner SFTP drop for daily CSV files.	Ch. 3, extraction
Object storage	MinIO	Holds staging, source-aligned, and quarantine zones.	Ch. 3, storage zones
Storage format	Apache Iceberg	Source-aligned Data Product tables, with ACID and time travel.	Ch. 3, format choice
Iceberg catalog	Apache Polaris	Catalog service for Iceberg tables, vendor-neutral.	Ch. 3, storage

Layer	Tool	What it does here	Concept from
Orchestration	Apache Airflow 2.9	One DAG per Data Product, task-based orchestration.	Ch. 3, orchestration
Managed connector	dlt	Batch and API extraction, Python-native.	Ch. 3, connectors
CDC framework	Debezium Server	Streams Postgres WAL changes to MinIO as JSON, no Kafka required.	Ch. 3, connectors
Quality gates	Soda Core	YAML rules for completeness, validity, uniqueness, freshness, volume.	Ch. 2, quality gates
Catalog and lineage	DataHub	Receives metadata sidecars, renders lineage, stores schema snapshots.	Ch. 2 and 3, metadata
Pipeline monitoring	Grafana	Reads Airflow's metadata DB, shows pipeline health and run history.	Ch. 3, monitoring

All of this is baked into the Docker files. I split it into two: a DataHub Docker (as DataHub itself already consumes a lot of other services) and the remaining stack.

A note on what we left out: We are not using Kafka, Spark, or dbt in this chapter. Not because they are bad choices in general, but because we do not need them here. Kafka is replaced by the Debezium Server, which writes directly to object storage. Spark is replaced by dlt and native Python, because the data volumes in this sample do not justify a distributed engine. dbt belongs to the integration phase, which is Volume 3.

Hardware. Plan for 16 GB of RAM, 4 CPU cores, and 20 GB of disk. DataHub and Airflow together account for most of the footprint.

Versions. All version numbers are pinned in the platform repository's Docker Compose file. They will drift over time. The concepts in this chapter do not depend on any specific version.

That is the stack. Now, let's look at how the repository is laid out before we start.

Repository layout and prerequisites

The platform repository (dp-book-v2) is the Docker Compose stack. Everything runs from here. You start this repository, and you have Postgres, MinIO, Airflow, Debezium Server, Polaris, Grafana, and the FastAPI dealer mock running on your laptop. DataHub has its own stack. The only thing we need is the token setup for DataHub; otherwise, the API isn't usable.

```
dp-book-v2/
├── README.md
├── docker-compose.yml
├── .env.example
├── config/
│   ├── airflow/
│   │   └── airflow.cfg
```

```
│   ├── debezium/
│   │   └── application.properties
│   ├── polaris/
│   │   └── bootstrap.sql
│   ├── datahub/
│   │   └── token-setup.sh
│   └── grafana/
│       └── dashboards/
│           └── pipeline-health.json
├── mocks/
│   └── dealer-api/
│       ├── Dockerfile
│       └── main.py
└── scripts/
    ├── seed-postgres.sh
    ├── seed-minio.sh
    └── wait-for-healthy.sh
```

A few things about this layout are worth mentioning.

The `.env.example` file contains all the environment variables you need: database passwords, MinIO access keys, the DataHub API token, and the Polaris admin credentials. Copy it to `.env`, fill in the blanks, and Compose reads it on startup. Never commit your filled-in `.env`. This is a critical security incident otherwise!

The `scripts/` directory holds three small bash scripts. `seed-postgres.sh` creates the MES schema and loads synthetic telemetry into Postgres. `seed-minio.sh` creates the buckets and uploads the supplier CSV files. `wait-for-healthy.sh` polls the health endpoints of every service and reports which ones are up. The stack takes three to four minutes to fully start, and DataHub in particular is slow on first boot.

The Data Product repository

These are the three Data Products. It assumes the platform repository is running. Don't start this before everything else is up and running! In the provided sample, we only have supplier quality. Please also note that I would rather recommend one repo per product, but for learning purposes, I pulled them into one.

```
dp-book-v2-mcc/
├── README.md
├── products/
│   ├── supplier-quality/
│   │   ├── odps.yaml
│   │   ├── soda-rules.yaml
│   │   ├── dag.py
│   │   └── retention.yaml
│   ├── dealer-service/
│   │   ├── odps.yaml
│   │   ├── soda-rules.yaml
│   │   ├── dag.py
│   │   └── retention.yaml
│   └── manufacturing-telemetry/
│       ├── odps.yaml
│       ├── soda-rules.yaml
│       ├── dag.py
│       ├── debezium.properties
│       └── retention.yaml
├── shared/
│   ├── pipeline_template.py
│   ├── classification.py
│   └── metadata_emitter.py
└── governance/
    ├── source_profiles/
    │   ├── supplier-quality.md
    │   ├── dealer-service.md
    │   └── manufacturing-telemetry.md
    └── collaboration_agreements/
        └── manufacturing-team.md
```

This layout is the book's thesis, made concrete. Each Data Product is its own folder with its own ODPS YAML, quality rules, DAG, and retention policy. Nothing about one product is buried inside another. The `shared/` folder holds the pipeline template, the classification logic, and the metadata emitter that every DAG imports. Governance documents live under `governance/`, in plain Markdown, so they can be reviewed in pull requests.

The synthetic data package

From the download link at the beginning of this chapter, you get `data.zip`. Unzip it somewhere convenient. It contains:

```
data/
├── supplier-quality/
│   ├── 2026-05-12.csv
│   ├── 2026-05-13.csv
│   └── ... (30 days of files)
├── dealer-service/
│   └── tickets.json        (loaded into the FastAPI
mock on startup)
└── manufacturing-telemetry/
    └── telemetry.sql       (loaded into Postgres on
startup)
```

Three Docker details that matter

The seed scripts in the platform repository assume the data/ folder is at a known location. Now let's have a look at some key aspects in the Docker file:

1: Debezium Server, configured to write directly to MinIO.

```
debezium-server:
  image: debezium/server:2.5
  depends_on:
    postgres:
      condition: service_healthy
    minio:
      condition: service_healthy
  volumes:
    -
./config/debezium/application.properties:/debezium/
config/application.properties
  environment:
    DEBEZIUM_SINK_TYPE: http
    DEBEZIUM_SINK_HTTP_URL:  http://minio:9000/cdc-
events
```

This is the single-binary mode of Debezium, with no Kafka, Kafka Connect, or Zookeeper. The application.properties file mounted at /debezium/config/ tells it to watch the mes database's WAL and write each change event as a JSON document to MinIO. The resulting files land in a bucket that Airflow picks up on its next run.

2: Polaris, bootstrapped with the Iceberg catalog for MCC.

```
polaris:
  image: apache/polaris:latest
  depends_on:
    postgres:
      condition: service_healthy
  ports:
    - "8181:8181"
  volumes:
```

```
    -
./config/polaris/bootstrap.sql:/opt/polaris/bootstr
ap.sql
  environment:
    POLARIS_PERSISTENCE: postgres
    POLARIS_BOOTSTRAP_CREDENTIALS:
${POLARIS_ADMIN_USER}:${POLARIS_ADMIN_SECRET}
```

Polaris stores its own catalog metadata in Postgres (the same instance that holds MES telemetry, in separate databases). The bootstrap.sql file creates the mcc catalog and three namespaces, one per Data Product. After the stack is up, Airflow DAGs use the Polaris REST API to create Iceberg tables inside those namespaces.

3: DataHub, with the API token generated on startup.

```
datahub-gms:
  image: acryldata/datahub-gms:latest
  depends_on:
    - datahub-upgrade
  environment:
    METADATA_SERVICE_AUTH_ENABLED: "true"
    DATAHUB_SYSTEM_TOKEN: ${DATAHUB_SYSTEM_TOKEN}
  volumes:
    - ./config/datahub/token-setup.sh:/docker-
entrypoint-init.d/token-setup.sh
```

This is the item that matters most. DataHub's API must be authenticated from the first run, because every pipeline pushes metadata through it. The token-setup.sh script runs during the first boot, creates a personal access token, and writes it to a shared volume that Airflow reads on startup. Do not skip this. Retrofitting authentication into a running DataHub instance is painful and has cost me entire afternoons. But be careful here, you should not do it this way in production (writing the PAT to a shared storage!).

The three source systems

Before we define the three Data Products, we profile the three sources. Chapter 2 argued that profiling precedes connecting and introduced the seven-dimension scorecard.

The data I used here was generated with mostly.ai.[2] Their Synthetic Data SDK is an open-source Python library (Apache 2.0 licensed) for generating synthetic data. I can recommend this to everyone who wants to build data that is modeled around real-world use cases without the risk of PII-related issues.

The profiles below describe what the MCC data team observed during a week spent with each source. The observations are real: every null rate, row count, and date range comes from the synthetic data package you downloaded before.

Profile 1: Supplier quality

Daily CSV files delivered by 25 parts suppliers to an SFTP drop bucket owned by MCC's procurement IT team. Each file contains one row for each inspected batch on that day. Files land between

[2] Mostly.ai: https://mostly.ai/.

07:30 and 08:30 in the morning, and the pipeline picks them up starting at 09:00. The format has not changed in two years, although the team confirms that the current column set was agreed only verbally and is not documented anywhere.

What we observed across 60 days

17,344 rows in total, averaging 289 rows per day, spanning 2026-03-12 to 2026-05-10. Twenty-five distinct suppliers, each sending between 2 and 35 rows per day, depending on their delivery schedule. 150 distinct part numbers. Inspection results break down roughly as 89% pass, 7% conditional pass, and 4% fail, which is consistent with what Klaus, the receiving inspector who serves as our Domain Expert for this source, describes as "a normal month."

Three observations stood out during profiling

First, on 2026-04-14, the file contained 836 rows, which was above the ~289-row average. A three-fold volume spike. The procurement IT team confirmed that this was the day three suppliers consolidated a backlog of delayed items into a single delivery. It was not a pipeline error. It was a real operational event. For our profile, this is useful: it tells us the source can legitimately produce volume surges on known reconciliation days, which means our volume gate needs to accommodate planned spikes rather than treat every surge as a failure.

Second, the `defect_count` field is null on 1.87% of rows. Inspecting the affected rows showed no pattern by supplier, part, or date. Klaus explained that some suppliers occasionally deliver batches without a QC report attached, and receiving inspectors then leave the field blank rather than guess. For our profile, this means the field is semantically optional at the source, even though it is operationally important for us. We will need a soft gate on null rate, not a hard gate.

The `inspector_notes` field is null on 37% of rows. This is not a data quality problem. It is simply that most batches do not warrant a note. Klaus writes one only when something is unusual. Empty is the normal state.

Third, the `batch_id` field contains 32 organic duplicates across the 60-day window. Klaus and the procurement IT team explained that some suppliers reuse internal batch identifiers across calendar months for partial-shipment scenarios. This is real-world behavior, not a data quality defect. Our profile needs to treat `batch_id` uniqueness as a soft gate, issuing a warning for duplicates rather than rejecting them.

Seven-dimension scorecard

Dimension	Score	Observation
Data quality baseline	7	Null rates are modest and explicable. A small number of organic duplicates on batch_id from supplier-side reuse. Categorical fields are consistent. defect_count nulls are semantically meaningful rather than dirty.
Schema stability	5	No schema change in two years. But the format is verbally agreed, not documented. A supplier-side change would arrive without warning.

Dimension	Score	Observation
Volume and growth	6	~17k rows over 60 days is tractable. Legitimate volume spikes (day 34) indicate a non-trivial upper bound. Growth is roughly flat.
Freshness and availability	8	Files land daily between 07:30 and 08:30. The window is reliable. Missed days are rare and explained (supplier holidays).
Technical accessibility	6	SFTP-style drop into MinIO is trivial to read. No streaming, no API complexity, but also no CDC option. Batch-only.
Ownership and contact	5	Procurement IT owns the SFTP bucket. Suppliers own the file contents. Split ownership across an external boundary complicates change management.
Compliance profile	5	No personal data. Supplier agreements are confidential commercial terms but the data itself is operational quality. Internal classification is appropriate.

Overall: **42 out of 70.**

The weaknesses are the split ownership across a vendor boundary and the undocumented schema. Both are known problems that surface in every one of Klaus's morning standups.

Observed schema, documented here because Volume 2 does not yet write Data Contracts.

Column	Type	Null rate	Notes
supplier_id	string	0%	25 distinct values, stable.
batch_qty	long	0%	Quantity of parts in the batch.
part_no	string	0%	150 distinct values.
batch_id	string	0%	32 organic duplicates from supplier-side reuse.

Column	Type	Null rate	Notes
received_date	date	0%	Normally equals the file date.
defect_count	integer	1.87%	Semantically optional at source.
pass_fail	string	0%	Three values: pass, conditional_pass, fail.
inspector_notes	string	37.1%	Free text, only filled when unusual.
defect_code	string	0%	Standardized defect code from the supplier QC system.
batch_weight_kg	double	0%	Total batch weight in kilograms.
defect_category	string	0%	Higher-level grouping of defect codes.
inspector_id	string	0%	Identifier of the receiving inspector at MCC.
_source_file	string	0%	Added by the pipeline. Source CSV filename, kept for lineage.

This table belongs in the source profile, not in the ODPS YAML. Volume 3 will elevate it to a formal Data Contract at the input port.

What the profile tells us we will need to do:

- A soft gate on `defect_count` null rate: warn above 1%, fail above 3%.
- A soft gate on `batch_id` uniqueness. The profile observed 32 organic duplicates across the 60-day window. Warn rather than reject, because suppliers legitimately reuse batch identifiers across calendar months.

- A hard gate on `received_date` validity: must not be in the future. The profile did observe future-dated rows in the synthetic data, which the pipeline will correctly reject into quarantine.

- A soft gate on volume, wide enough to tolerate the observed variance with headroom. Suggested range: 100 to 3,000 rows per file.

- Hard not-null gates on `batch_id` and `supplier_id`. These two fields anchor every record and must always be present.

- A validity gate on `pass_fail`: allowed values are pass, conditional_pass, and fail. Anything else is treated as a row-level rejection.

- No freshness gate on individual files, because the file-date convention enforces freshness implicitly. But a freshness gate on "at least one file received in the last 36 hours" guards against missed deliveries.

We will write these as Soda rules when we build the Supplier pipeline.

Profile 2: Dealer service

What is the source?

MCC's Dealer Management System is exposed through an internal REST API. 60 dealers worldwide log service tickets against it. The API supports pagination (100 tickets per page) and an `updated_since` filter, which makes timestamp-based delta extraction straightforward. MCC's Aftersales IT team owns the API and has a published OpenAPI spec that is kept current.

What we observed.

40,120 tickets across 60 days (2026-03-12 to 2026-05-11). Twenty standardized complaint codes. Warranty claims on 26.8% of tickets, consistent with Aftersales' quarterly reports. The `replaced_part_number` field is null for 59.6% of tickets, which matches the real-world rate (most services do not replace parts). The `customer_comment` field is null for 39% of records and, when present, often contains names, phone numbers, or vehicle locations. This is the PII risk we flagged earlier.

One anomaly: 120 tickets share `ticket_id` with another ticket, typically on an adjacent `service_date`. Sara, the API product owner, confirmed this happens when a dealer's local system retries a POST after a network timeout. The API does not currently deduplicate on the write path. For us, this means we cannot trust `ticket_id` as unique and must enforce it at retrieval.

Seven-dimension scorecard

Dimension	Score	Observation
Data quality baseline	7	Null rates match business reality. ticket_id duplicates are known and bounded.

Dimension	Score	Observation
Schema stability	8	OpenAPI spec, versioned, communicated changes. Strongest schema discipline of the three sources.
Volume and growth	7	Predictable daily volume, gentle upward trend as the dealer network expands.
Freshness and availability	8	API is always up. updated_since filter guarantees no missed tickets if polling stays within the retention window.
Technical accessibility	9	Standard REST with pagination and delta filtering. Ideal for a managed connector.
Ownership and contact	7	Single owner team, responsive, holds a weekly sync with data consumers.
Compliance profile	5	customer_comment contains PII. GDPR applies. Source classification is Confidential.

Overall: 51 out of 70. The strongest source of the three. The only real concern is the PII in free-text comments.

Observed schema

Column	Type	Null rate	Notes
ticket_id	string	0%	Unique except for the ~120 duplicate cases.
vin	string	0%	17-char VIN, overlaps with Manufacturing Telemetry pool.
dealer_id	string	0%	60 distinct values.
service_date	date	0%	Within last 60 days.
complaint_code	string	0%	20 standardized codes.
replaced_part_number	string	59.6%	When present, overlaps with Supplier Quality pool.
labor_hours	decimal(4,2)	0%	Range 0.25 to 8.00.

Column	Type	Null rate	Notes
customer_comment	string	39.0%	Free text, PII-bearing.
warranty_claim	boolean	0%	26.8% true.
api_retrieved_at	timestamp	0%	API response timestamp.

What the profile tells us we will need to do.

- Hard gate on `ticket_id` uniqueness within each hourly pull, with deduplication logic in the classification stage.
- Hard gate on `vin` format (17 chars, no I/O/Q).
- Soft gate on `customer_comment` null rate, because a sudden drop to near zero might indicate a dealer frontend change.
- Pattern-based classification on `customer_comment` to tag PII for downstream handling.
- Freshness gate: most recent `api_retrieved_at` must be within 2 hours.

Profile 3: Manufacturing telemetry

You should now already know the drill. I will shorten this section a bit as it is repetitive from the previous two.

The MCC Manufacturing Execution System runs on PostgreSQL 16. It records one row per station event on the assembly line: 40

stations, 150 operators across three shifts, roughly 3,300 events per day weighted to working hours. The MES was installed in 2017 and was never intended as a data source. There is no API and no export mechanism.

The only viable extraction path is CDC against the Write-Ahead Log via Debezium Server, which requires negotiating access with the manufacturing operations team that owns the infrastructure.

Across the 60-day profiling window, we observed 199,345 events, a 97.9% pass rate, and one two-hour gap on 2026-04-21 that turned out to be planned maintenance. The sensor and operator fields are null by design (station-dependent for sensors, unmanned stations for operators), which is structural, not a quality problem.

The scorecard tells the real story of this source, and every subsequent activity in the chapter traces back to it. The low scores on schema stability, technical accessibility, and ownership are the reasons we need a collaboration agreement, high-sensitivity schema drift detection, and a freshness gate paired with a maintenance calendar. Nothing about this Data Product is accidental. Every architectural and governance decision is a direct response to a specific weakness the scorecard surfaces.

Seven-dimension scorecard

Dimension	Score	Observation	Consequence for the Data Product
Data quality baseline	6	Consistent categorical values, explicable null patterns, no orphan records against shared VIN pool.	Soft gates sufficient. Structural nulls accepted without flagging.
Schema stability	4	MES team deploys quarterly with little to no prior notice. Column renames observed historically. No published schema contract.	High-sensitivity schema snapshot on every run. Drift detection is the first thing the pipeline checks.
Volume and growth	6	Highest volume of the three sources at ~200k rows / 60 days. Flat growth today, but planned line expansions for 2027 could double the rate.	Iceberg partitioning by event date. Pipeline sized for 2x headroom.
Freshness and availability	5	Continuous under normal operation. Planned maintenance windows (1–4 hours) occur on no fixed schedule. Unplanned stops are rare but happen.	1-hour freshness gate paired with a maintenance calendar pushed by the MES team. Without the calendar, the gate pages the on-call engineer for every planned stop.
Technical accessibility	4	No API, no batch export. Only WAL-based CDC is feasible. Requires PostgreSQL logical replication to be enabled and a replication slot to be maintained.	Debezium Server as the connector. Snapshot-then-streaming mode. Dedicated replication slot owned by our team, monitored for lag.

Dimension	Score	Observation	Consequence for the Data Product
Ownership and contact	5	Manufacturing operations owns the MES. They are responsive but do not see themselves as a data source owner. No existing relationship with downstream consumers.	The collaboration agreement later in this chapter is the instrument that formalizes this relationship. Without it, schema changes continue to arrive unannounced.
Compliance profile	8	No personal data. operator_id is a work identifier tied to a shift badge, not a personal identifier. Internal classification appropriate.	Standard retention tier. No masking, anonymization, or column-level lineage needed.

Overall: 38 out of 70. The weakest source of the three. The score reflects a real truth: the MES was not designed for us, and closing that gap is a multi-quarter program, not a Data Product deliverable.

With all three sources profiled, we can make the decisions that the profiles set up. The first of those is classification.

Classification decisions

Classification is the decision we make based on the scorecard. We defined four classification levels (Public, Internal, Confidential, Restricted) and argued that classification should happen at ingestion, not retroactively.

For MCC's three sources, the decisions are straightforward once the profiles are on the table.

Data Product	Classification	Primary reason	Governance consequences
Supplier Quality	Internal	Commercial quality data, no personal data. Supplier agreements are confidential but the data itself is operational.	Standard retention. No masking. Internal access via role-based permissions.
Dealer Service	Confidential	customer_comment contains PII (names, phone numbers, vehicle locations). GDPR applies.	Extended retention with anonymization after 24 months. Pattern-based PII detection at classification stage. Column-level lineage for customer_comment.
Manufacturing Telemetry	Internal	Operational telemetry. operator_id is a work identifier, not a personal one.	Standard retention. No masking. Internal access.

The classification label is attached as metadata at the classification stage of the pipeline. From that moment onward, it travels with the data and drives every downstream governance decision: access control, retention tier, masking, and lineage granularity.

Collaboration agreement: The manufacturing team

The Manufacturing Telemetry profile scored 5 on ownership and 4 on schema stability. Both numbers point to the same problem: the MES team is responsive when asked, but does not see itself as a data source owner. Schema changes arrive without notice. Maintenance windows are not communicated to downstream consumers. Access depends on personal relationships rather than a defined process.

Chapter 4 argued that the instrument for fixing this is a lightweight collaboration agreement. Not a data contract, which the MES team would not sign and cannot be meaningfully enforced against a system they did not build to be a data source. A people agreement, covering five things. Here is what the actual MCC document looks like.

The agreement lives at `governance/collaboration_agreements/manufacturing-team.md` in the Data Product repository, in plain Markdown, and is reviewed and updated through pull requests, like any other governance artifact.

```
# Collaboration Agreement: Manufacturing Telemetry
Source

**Between:** MCC Data Products team (Manufacturing
Telemetry squad)
**And:**     MCC Manufacturing Operations (MES
infrastructure team)
**Effective:** 2026-05-15
**Review cadence:** Quarterly
```

1. Contact list

MES side
- Technical contact: Tomás Ferreira (MES admin, schema and replication slot questions)
- Escalation: Ingrid Holm (Manufacturing Operations lead)

Data Products side
- Technical contact: Sofia Lindgren (Data Engineer, Manufacturing Telemetry squad)
- Accountable: Maria Chen (Data Product Owner)

Slack channel for day-to-day: `#mes-data-products`.

2. Change notification commitment

The MES team will notify the Data Products team at least 5 working days before any change that affects:

- Column additions, renames, removals, type changes in `mes.telemetry`
- Replication slot reconfiguration
- PostgreSQL version upgrades
- Changes to the MES deployment cadence

Notification goes to `#mes-data-products` and creates a ticket in the
Data Products team's board.

Emergency changes (security patches, outages) are exempt from the 5-day
notice but must be communicated as soon as possible, same day.

3. Maintenance window schedule

Planned MES maintenance windows are published by the MES team to
`governance/maintenance_calendars/mes.yaml` in the Data Product repo.
Windows in that file are excluded from freshness alerting automatically.

Windows not published in that file will generate an alert when the
freshness gate fires, and the Data Products on-call engineer will reach
out to Tomás for context.

```
## 4. Data quality baseline acknowledgment

Both teams acknowledge the source profile at
`governance/source_profiles/manufacturing-
telemetry.md` as the shared
baseline. Specifically:

- Null rate 35.4% on `operator_id` is structural
(unmanned stations)
- Pass rate ~97% is the normal operating range
- Scheduled maintenance creates freshness gaps, see
section 3

If any of these baselines shift materially, the MES
team will flag it
through the same channel as a schema change.

## 5. Escalation path

When an issue arises that cannot be resolved between
Tomás and Sofia:

1. Maria (Data Product Owner) and Ingrid (Manufacturing
Operations lead)
2. If still unresolved, escalation to the CDO office
and the Manufacturing
   Operations director

The goal is always to resolve at level 1. Escalation
is a backstop, not
a first move.

---
Last reviewed: 2026-05-15
Next review:  2026-08-15
Signed (digital): Maria Chen, Ingrid Holm
```

The benefit of this approach is clear: the collaboration agreement sits version-controlled in Git. When something in this contract changes, we can track it over time. There is no need to do a long-tail email chain analysis of what was eventually agreed upon.

The other two sources (Supplier Quality, Dealer Service) have similar agreements, written against their respective profiles. We do not reproduce them here. They are shorter because the underlying relationships are less strained. The supplier's agreement focuses on the file-drop schedule and the handling of late deliveries. The dealer's agreement is nearly ceremonial, since Sara's team already holds a weekly sync with data consumers, and most of the five points are standard practice.

With the three profiles documented, the classifications decided, and the collaboration agreements in place, we are ready to formally define the Data Products. That is what we do next.

Defining the three Data Products with ODPS

Now that we have the infrastructure and the repository layout, we will write the source of truth for each Data Product. One ODPS YAML per product, committed to the Data Product repository under `products/<name>/odps.yaml`.

As we noted in the introduction to this book, Data Contracts are a Volume 3 topic. In this chapter, every contractId in each YAML file is a placeholder pointing to a contract that will be written in Volume 3. Everything else is real.

We will write the Supplier Quality YAML in full because it is the pipeline we walk through in depth later in the chapter. The other two we compress into blocks that differ by Supplier. The complete versions of all three live in the Data Product repository.

The full supplier quality YAML


```
apiVersion: v1.0.0
kind: DataProduct
status: draft
id: 3f8b2e90-5d1c-4a7f-b8e3-9c2a1f6d4e80
version: v1.0.0
name: Supplier Quality
domain: Quality
tenant: MCC

description:
  purpose: >
    Source-aligned Data Product exposing batch-level
quality data
    received from parts suppliers. Captures defect
rates, inspection
    results, and receiving inspector notes for every
incoming batch.
  limitations: >
    Volume 2 scope. No integration with dealer
service or manufacturing
    telemetry yet. Aggregated defect analytics will
be provided by a
    separate Data Product in Volume 3.
  usage: >
    Consumed by downstream Quality Intelligence
products for early
    detection of supplier-side quality drift. Not
intended for direct
    consumption by business users.

inputPorts:
  - name: supplier-csv-drop
    version: v1.0.0
    description: Daily CSV files delivered by
suppliers to the MCC drop bucket
    contractId: TBD-VOLUME-3
    tags:
      - batch
      - daily
      - partner-delivered
```

```yaml
    customProperties:
      - property: sourceSystem
        value: MCC-SUPPLIER-SFTP
      - property: sourceProfileRef
        value: products/supplier-
quality/source_profile.md
      - property: extractionPattern
        value: file-based-batch
      - property: connectorTool
        value: dlt

outputPorts:
  - name: supplier-quality-bronze
    version: v1.0.0
    description: Source-aligned Iceberg table with
validated supplier batches
    type: iceberg-table
    location: mcc.quality.supplier_quality_bronze
    contractId: TBD-VOLUME-3
    tags:
      - source-aligned
      - bronze
      - classified-internal
    customProperties:
      - property: storageFormat
        value: iceberg
      - property: storageBackend
        value: minio
      - property: catalogService
        value: polaris
      - property: retentionTier
        value: standard

authoritativeDefinitions:
  - type: source-profile
    url: products/supplier-
quality/source_profile.md
  - type: collaboration-agreement
    url: products/supplier-
quality/collaboration_agreement.md
  - type: retention-policy
    url: products/supplier-quality/retention.yaml

support:
  - channel: "#data-quality-supplier"
    url: https://mcc.slack.com/archives/data-
quality-supplier
    tool: slack
    scope: interactive
```

```
  - channel: quality-data-oncall
    url: mailto:quality-data-oncall@mcc.example
    tool: email
    scope: issues

team:
  name: Supplier Quality squad
  members:
    - username: maria.chen@mcc.example
      name: Maria Chen
      role: Data Product Owner
    - username: raj.patel@mcc.example
      name: Raj Patel
      role: Tech Lead
    - username: sofia.lindgren@mcc.example
      name: Sofia Lindgren
      role: Data Engineer
    - username: klaus.weber@mcc.example
      name: Klaus Weber
      role: Domain Expert

tags:
  - quality
  - supplier
  - source-aligned
  - classification:internal

productCreatedTs: 2026-05-10T09:00:00Z

customProperties:
  - property: sourceProfileScore
    value: 42
  - property: classificationLevel
    value: Internal
  - property: volume3Ready
    value: false
```

A few things in this YAML are worth naming explicitly.

The `id` is a UUID, not a number. ODPS allows either. Using a UUID eliminates the risk of collisions across organizations or tenants, and it survives renames. If we ever decide "Supplier Quality" should be called something else, the name changes, the UUID does not.

The two `contractId` fields are placeholders. The input port's contract will describe what we expect the supplier CSVs to contain. The output port's contract will describe what our Bronze Iceberg table guarantees to downstream consumers. Both are Volume 3 work. Leaving them as literal `TBD-VOLUME-3` strings is ok: a CI validation rule in the repository can fail the build if any production ODPS YAML still contains that string, which forces the team to come back and fill them in when the contracts are written.

The `authoritativeDefinitions` block points outward. Source profile, collaboration agreement, and retention policy. Three separate files, each with its own purpose, each versioned in Git alongside the YAML. This is ODPS doing its job properly: the YAML does not try to be the whole truth; it points at the documents that are.

The `customProperties` block contains MCC-specific information not included in the standard. The source profile score from Chapter 2's seven-dimension scorecard. The classification level. A `volume3Ready` flag that can be flipped to `true` once contracts exist. Custom properties are the correct extension mechanism for organizational additions to ODPS, and using them keeps the standard-compliant parts of the YAML clean.

The names in the `team` block are illustrative. For your real Data Products, these are the people accountable for the retrieval activities we mapped in Chapter 4 of the RACI. The Data Product Owner is accountable for governance decisions. The Tech Lead owns the architectural calls. The Data Engineer does the work. The Domain Expert provides the business context that nobody else can. All four are named in the YAML because all four are needed.

Dealer Service and Manufacturing Telemetry, compressed

We won't go into a full listing of the other two ODPS definitions. You can look them up in the Git repository. I'll list the most important differences here for your reference.

Three things differ from Supplier for the dealer service. The domain is `Aftersales`, not `Quality`. The classification is `Confidential` rather than `Internal`, because customer comments in service tickets can contain personal data. The extraction pattern is `timestamp-based-delta` over an API, not a file-based batch. Everything else, including the team structure, support block, and authoritative definitions pattern, follows the Supplier template.

Manufacturing Telemetry has the highest volume and the lowest source profile score of the three. The score of 38 reflects the realities captured in the Chapter 2 scorecard: the MES was never designed to be a data source, so technical accessibility is limited to WAL-based CDC, schema stability is moderate, and ownership is shared across the manufacturing operations team. The Data Product still works. The profile score simply tells future readers of the YAML that this source needs more operational attention than the others.

What the three YAMLs give us

Taken together, the three YAMLs are now the shared source of truth for every downstream system. The DataHub catalog can be populated from them. The Airflow DAGs can be parameterized from them, retention policies can be triggered from them, and classification labels can be enforced from them. When anything changes about a Data Product, the YAML changes first, and every other system follows.

This is the Chapter 1 principle, turned into three concrete files.

The Data Product repository after this step

Three YAMLs committed, with their governance artifacts sitting next to them. The repository now looks like this.

```
dp-book-v2-mcc/
├── README.md
├── products/
│   ├── supplier-quality/
│   │   ├── odps.yaml
│   │   ├── retention.yaml
│   │   ├── source_profile.md
│   │   └── collaboration_agreement.md
│   ├── dealer-service/
│   │   ├── odps.yaml
│   │   ├── retention.yaml
│   │   ├── source_profile.md
```

```
|   |   └── collaboration_agreement.md
|   └── manufacturing-telemetry/
|       ├── odps.yaml
|       ├── retention.yaml
|       ├── source_profile.md
|       └── collaboration_agreement.md
```

The pipelines in practice

Now let's have a look at the different pipelines and how they match. We start with the shared pipeline template to ensure reusability across all aspects of the work we do within the organization.

The shared pipeline template

We are building three Data Products. If each one had its own pipeline implementation, written from scratch, we would end up with three subtly different ways of doing the same five things: extracting, staging, validating, classifying, and loading data. Three implementations mean three places to fix every bug, three places to update when DataHub changes its API, and three different conventions to learn before you can work on someone else's product.

This is a real failure mode. I have seen teams of six engineers maintain twelve pipelines where every pipeline did the same five things twelve subtly different ways. Onboarding took weeks. Incident response was a per-pipeline detective exercise. Schema changes that should have taken one pull request took twelve.

The shared template solves this by inverting the relationship. The template defines the shape of every Data Product retrieval pipeline. Per-product files define the content: what to extract, which Soda rules to run, and where to write. The template imports the content at runtime via a plug-in mechanism. Three Data Products, one orchestration file, three small per-product files. See Figure 9 for the sample!

Every retrieval pipeline runs the same seven tasks in the same topology: extract, stage, validate, then a parallel branch into classify and quarantine, joining back at load, and ending with emit_metadata. The quarantine branch is smaller, as this is the rejection path.

The shape is enforced by shared/pipeline_template.py. The function that wires it up is build_retrieval_pipeline(dag, product_config). The wiring itself is two lines of Airflow operator syntax:

```
extract >> stage >> validate

validate >> [classify, quarantine]

classify >> load >> emit_metadata
```

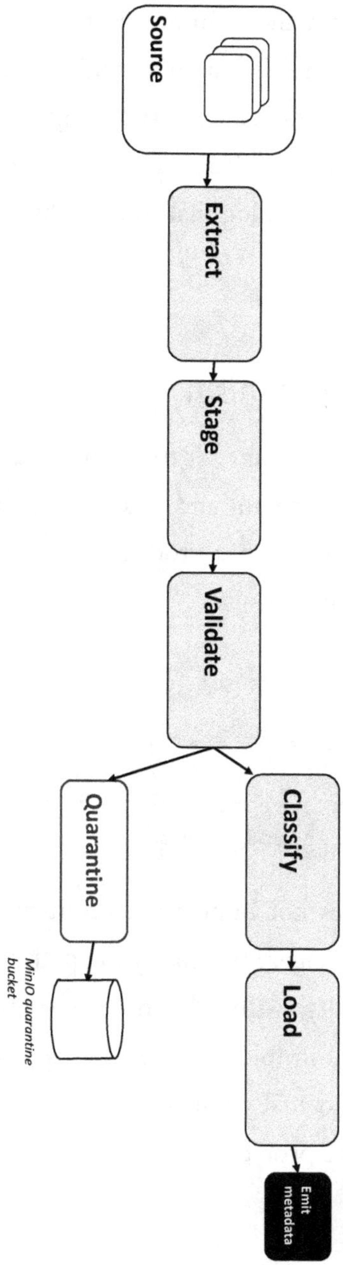

Figure 9: The shared retrieval pipeline template.

Read it left to right. Validate branches into classify and quarantine in parallel. Classify feeds load. Quarantine writes to MinIO and stops. The emit_metadata task runs regardless of whether the pipeline succeeded or failed, because we want failed runs in DataHub as well. A catalog that hides failures is worse than one that records them.

The plug-in mechanism

The six stage functions (extract_fn, stage_fn, validate_fn, classify_fn, quarantine_fn, and load_fn) are not defined in the template. They live in a per-product stages.py and are loaded at runtime by file path:

```
spec =
 importlib.util.spec_from_file_location(name,
stages_module_path)
module = importlib.util.module_from_spec(spec)
spec.loader.exec_module(module)
```

The template does not import the product; the product is not imported as a package. Loading by file path means folder names like supplier-quality (with a hyphen) work without translation. Hyphens are valid in folder names, URLs, and DataHub URNs. They are not valid in Python module names. Loading by path sidesteps the entire problem.

What a per-product DAG file contains

For each Data Product, the team writes one short DAG file. It contains exactly three things:

1. A PRODUCT_CONFIG dictionary with the product's identifier, classification level, output port location, and the absolute path to its stages.py.
2. An Airflow DAG context with its dag_id, schedule, and tags.
3. A single call to build_retrieval_pipeline(dag, PRODUCT_CONFIG).

The Supplier Quality DAG file is 44 lines, including imports and blank lines. The Dealer Service file is structurally identical with different identifiers. Same for Manufacturing Telemetry. When a new Data Product is added, this is the file the team writes from scratch. Everything else is borrowed from the template.

What this buys the team

Three things, roughly in order of impact.

Consistency. Every retrieval pipeline has the same task topology, the same naming, and the same metadata emission. When an engineer is paged at 03:15 because a pipeline failed, they do not have to remember which product uses which conventions. The DAG view in Airflow looks the same across all products. The failure path is the same. The recovery procedure is the same.

One place to evolve the platform. When DataHub releases a new metadata API version, the change happens in shared/metadata_emitter.py once, and all three pipelines pick it up. When we want to add a common task between validate and classify, such as schema drift detection, we add it to the template, and all three pipelines inherit it. When we hit the pyiceberg nanosecond-timestamp limitation that the next section covers, the fix lives in a single shared utility, not in three separate stage files.

A clear contract for what a retrieval pipeline does. The template is the contract. If your stages.py file does not include all six functions, the DAG fails to load. Missing functions are caught at DAG-load time, not in production at 03:15. The platform fails closed.

There is one thing the template does not buy us. It does not give us access to the interesting part of each Data Product. The extraction logic, the quality rules, the classification specifics, and the load semantics. Those still have to be written, thought about, and reviewed individually. The next section walks through exactly that for Supplier Quality.

Pipeline 1: Supplier Quality batch, in full

The Supplier Quality pipeline is the anchor of this chapter. Dealer Service and Manufacturing Telemetry use the same template, the same shared utilities, and the same DataHub emission. This section walks through what is specific to Supplier, where the design decisions from Chapters 1 through 3 land in actual code, and which technical realities surprised us during the build. The full source lives in the repo at dp-book-v2-mcc/products/supplier-quality/. I will not show every line of code in the pipeline, as this would greatly extend the book's content. Instead, I will show some key insights from the code.

What the pipeline actually does

In the Supplier case, the source is 60 daily CSV files in a MinIO bucket. The output port is one Iceberg table, mcc.quality.supplier_quality_bronze, classified as Internal. Between the two: read, validate, classify, quarantine future-dated rows, and load.

In a single run, the pipeline reads 60 CSV files containing 17,344 rows. It quarantines 20 of them (future-dated) and loads 17,324 to Iceberg. Soda evaluates five quality rules; two of them warn (1.87% null on defect_count, 32 organic duplicates on batch_id) and three pass. Classification flags 216 PII matches across all rows for downstream awareness. DataHub records the run, the lineage, and the schema snapshot. Total runtime: about 19 seconds.

That is the work. The interesting question is how each Chapter 2 and 3 design decision shows up in the code.

Extract: dlt against MinIO

The extraction stage uses dlt to read CSVs from MinIO. The decision was a managed connector for file-based batch sources, not custom Python. dlt is the managed connector. The actual extract function declares a filesystem source, points it at the bucket, and returns a DataFrame:

```
def supplier_csv_source(bucket: str, prefix: str =
"supplier-drop/"):
    return
filesystem(bucket_url=f"s3://{bucket}/{prefix}",
file_glob="*.csv") | read_csv()
```

The function returns a dlt resource, which the pipeline materializes into a DataFrame in the staging step. The full extract function adds standard logging and a _source_file column for lineage, but the data flow is as shown above. One source declaration, one CSV reader, and dlt handles iteration across files.

Two things worth knowing about this. First, dlt assumes the CSVs share a schema. If a supplier adds or renames a column on day 38, dlt will either crash or drop the difference, depending on the configuration. The source profile assumes a stable schema, and the collaboration agreement makes the supplier-IT team responsible for advance notice. The pipeline trusts that agreement. The schema snapshot emitted to DataHub gives us evidence after the fact if the trust is broken.

Second, the s3:// URL format is incompatible with MinIO because it is S3-compatible at the protocol level. The dlt code does not care that the storage is local. The endpoint URL is set in environment variables. This is a small thing that comes up in every open-source stack: cloud APIs are everywhere, even where the cloud isn't.

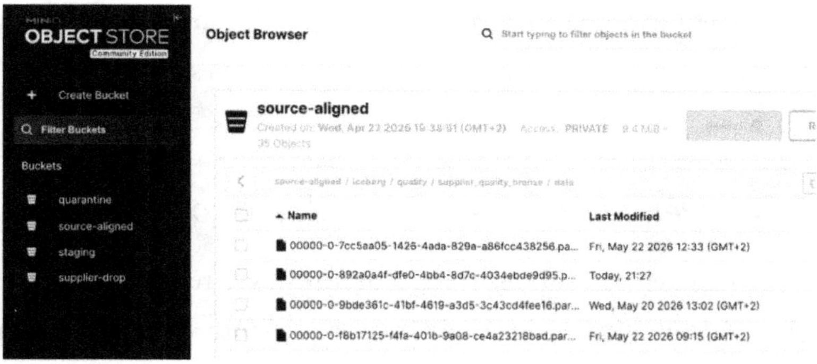

Figure 10: The Data in Minio.

Validate: Soda Core via DuckDB

The validation stage reads the staged Parquet, runs a Soda Core scan, and decides which rows to keep. The Soda rules file is small enough to show:

```
checks for supplier_quality:
  - missing_percent(defect_count):
      warn: when > 1
      fail: when > 3
  - duplicate_count(batch_id):
      warn: when > 0
  - missing_count(batch_id) = 0
  - missing_count(supplier_id) = 0
  - invalid_count(pass_fail) = 0:
      valid values: [pass, conditional_pass, fail]
```

The Soda scan runs against a DuckDB connection that treats the staged Parquet file as a table. This works because DuckDB can register Parquet files as views, and Soda Core can target any data source DuckDB exposes. No Postgres, no in-memory pandas tricks, no temporary tables. The staged Parquet is the table, DuckDB is the query engine, and Soda is the rules engine.

Row-level quarantine: future-dated rows

Soda handles batch-level rules. For row-level rejection, we use plain Python. The profile told us to expect future-dated rows in the data (planted by the synthetic data generator, but representative of real ingestion errors from suppliers with misconfigured clocks). The validate stage filters those out:

```
quarantine_mask = df["received_date"] > today
quarantined = df[quarantine_mask].copy()
quarantined["_quarantine_reason"] =
"validity.received_date.future"
good = df[~quarantine_mask]
```

Twenty rows are quarantined. They go to MinIO under quarantine/supplier-quality/<run_id>/, with one JSON file per row, preserving the rejection reason and the original payload. The good rows continue to be classified and loaded.

Row-level rejection is the design pattern I am most insistent on in the book. Hard batch-level rejection (rejecting the entire CSV file because a single row is bad) is operationally toxic. Either bad data flows through anyway because the team disables the gate after the third 03:15 page, or good data is held back for hours because of a single corrupted row. Row-level quarantine breaks the deadlock. Good rows continue but bad rows are preserved for investigation.

Load: Polaris and the timestamp-precision problem

The load stage writes good.parquet to Iceberg via a Polaris REST catalog client. The mechanics are short:

```
catalog = load_catalog("mcc", **polaris_rest_config)
table                                                    =
catalog.load_table("quality.supplier_quality_bronze
")
table.append(arrow_table)
```

One more detail about the load step is worth surfacing. The first time the pipeline runs, it creates the Iceberg table. On every subsequent run, it appends. If the Iceberg schema in Polaris differs from the DataFrame's schema (because, say, we added a new column upstream and forgot to migrate), pyiceberg raises a clear error. The pipeline fails closed rather than dropping the new column. That is the behavior we want.

Classify: PII detection without ML

The classify stage applies two things. First, the baseline classification level from product_config (in the Supplier's case, Internal). Second, a pattern-based PII scan over string columns. The PII detector is regex, not a machine learning model:

```
def detect_pii(value: str) -> list[str]:
    matches = []
    if                        EMAIL_RE.search(value):
matches.append("email")
    if                     PHONE_EU_RE.search(value):
matches.append("phone_eu")
    if                         NAME_RE.search(value):
matches.append("name_like")
    return matches
```

For Supplier, the PII detection finds 216 matches across the dataset, distributed mostly in inspector_notes (free-text field). For Dealer, the same detector finds far more, distributed in customer_comment. The matches are recorded as metadata against the dataset; they do not trigger any quarantine. The classification level in the dataset remains Internal for Supplier and Confidential for Dealer. Pattern matching rather than ML is the right tool for this scale. The dataset is bounded (tens of thousands of rows, dozens of patterns), the patterns are well-known (emails, EU phone formats, common name structures), and the false-positive rate is acceptable because the consequence of a false positive is a metadata flag, not a rejection. ML would be more accurate and far more expensive. For Bronze-level retrieval, this is the right trade.

Metadata emission: lineage and schema in DataHub

After load completes, emit_metadata calls emit_pipeline_run from shared/metadata_emitter.py. The emitter sends three MCPs (Metadata Change Proposals) to DataHub:

- dataProductProperties for the Data Product entity itself.
- upstreamLineage linking the Iceberg dataset back to its source URN (the MinIO CSV bucket, in the Supplier's case).
- schemaMetadata with the actual column list and types from the loaded Iceberg table.

What it looks like when the pipeline runs

A successful run produces four artifacts that the reader can see:

1. An Iceberg table at mcc.quality.supplier_quality_bronze with 17,324 rows and 13 columns.

2. 20 JSON files under quarantine/supplier-quality/<run_id>/ in MinIO, each with a _quarantine_reason of validity.received_date.future.

3. A Data Product entity in DataHub with lineage from the MinIO source URN to the Iceberg dataset URN, plus the schema snapshot.

4. A Grafana panel showing the run duration (~19 seconds), task durations per stage, row counts at each stage, and the Soda check outcomes.

Now that you understand how to build your pipelines, you can go ahead and create the other two. Not much changes between them, aside from the data sources. We keep the very same structure and reuse all shared templates across the services.

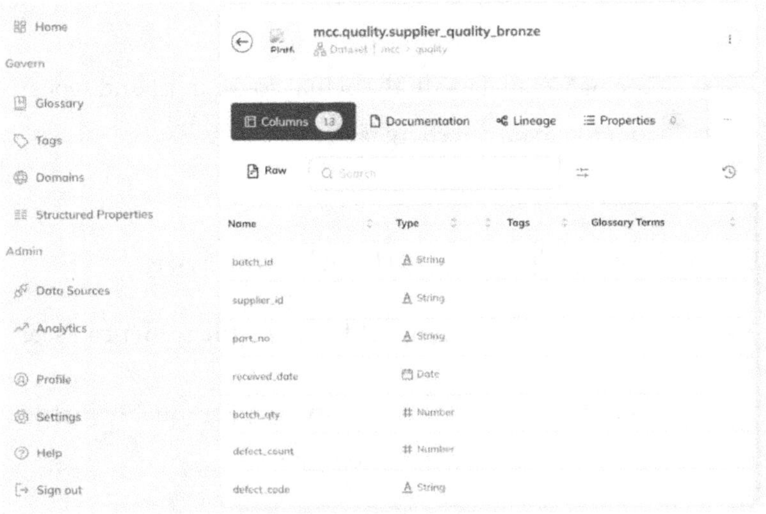

Figure 11: The Data Product in Datahub.

Anna's recall investigation, the one that opened this chapter, is still running in the fictional MCC. The Quality Intelligence team that will actually solve it does not exist yet. Building it is a Volume 3 problem. What we built in Chapter 5 is the floor that the team will stand on.

Three source-aligned Data Products: Supplier Quality, Dealer Service, Manufacturing Telemetry, with one shared platform: PostgreSQL, MinIO, Polaris, Airflow, Soda, DataHub, and Grafana. One template orchestrating three pipelines. One collaboration agreement with the Manufacturing team, which owns a system they did not build, to use as a data source. One classification scheme that travels with the data into the catalog.

The MCC sample is a worked example of how a Data Product can be built in an organization. Every choice in it, like the open-source stack, the file-then-API-then-CDC source mix, the narrow Manufacturing schema, the row-level quarantine pattern, and the regex-based PII detection, is one defensible answer to one set of constraints. Your constraints will differ. The shape that survives the differences is the shape the chapter has been pushing on: a Data Product is governance, architecture, and people together (GAP), and the source-aligned layer is where that shape first becomes real.

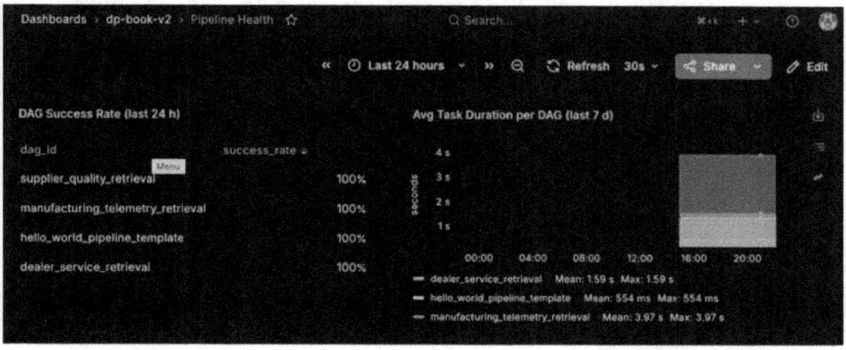

Figure 12: Monitoring Sample in Grafana.

Three things to remember from this chapter:

1. Source-aligned Data Products are not Bronze tables with a YAML on top. They are a contract between the team that knows the source and the team that consumes it. The pipelines in this chapter make that contract executable. The collaboration agreement, the source profile, the classification decision, and the metadata that

flows into DataHub are all part of the same artifact. You cannot build one without building the others.

2. The interesting work happens at the boundaries. The pyiceberg timestamp downcast, the DataHub schema validation, and the Soda API discovery. None of these are in vendor documentation; all of them appeared in a single chapter, based on a small, controlled sample. Build the boundary handling first; trust the center will be fine.

3. The platform's job is to disappear. When a new Data Product is added to MCC, the team writes one DAG file, one stages file, one Soda rules file, and three Markdown documents in the product folder. The template handles the rest. If the platform team ever has to be in the room when a new Data Product is added, the platform has failed.

What we did here on purpose was to avoid a vendor-specific stack. Databricks and Snowflake offer powerful capabilities, but this book was never about choosing one platform over the other. It was about the concept beneath the platform. The shape of a Data Product, the discipline of source profiling, the contract between teams, and the metadata that makes it all observable. None of that is vendor-specific, and none of it goes away when you switch tools.

Hiking is a useful analogy. Once you know what a long hike requires, such as route planning, weight management, weather windows, and knowing when to turn back, most mountains are open to you. You are not learning the mountain. You are learning yourself on the mountain. The next one looks different and behaves the same.

This book worked the same way. The stack we used was strictly ordinary: PostgreSQL, MinIO, Polaris, Airflow, Soda, DataHub, and Grafana. If you have a different stack tomorrow, the chapter you just read still applies. The source profile is the same artifact whether the source is an SFTP drop or a Snowflake share. The collaboration agreement is the same instrument whether the downstream platform is Databricks, Fabric, or something that does not exist yet. The classification level, the row-level quarantine pattern, and the schema snapshot in the catalog—all of it travels.

Take what you learned here and apply it to whatever your organization runs. Or to whatever it runs five years from now. The platform will change but the Data Product won't.

Index